YEARNING DESIRE FOR INTIMACY AND FULFILLMENT

YEARNING DESIRE FOR INTIMACY AND FULFILLMENT

Compassionate And Emotional Needs

Elder G. E. Johnson

iUniverse, Inc.
Bloomington

YEARNING DESIRE FOR INTIMACY AND FULFILLMENT
Compassionate And Emotional Needs

iUniverse books may be ordered through booksellers or by contacting:

iUniverse
1663 Liberty Drive
Bloomington, IN 47403
www.iuniverse.com
1-800-Authors (1-800-288-4677)

ISBN: 978-1-4620-2399-8 (pbk)
ISBN: 978-1-4620-2400-1 (ebk)

Printed in the United States of America

iUniverse rev. date: 07/12/2011

Contents

God furnishes us the ability to stand against these
divers temptation of the enemy.

The enjoyment of sex in marriage is appropriate and
should be pleasurable.

People who expect to be happy everyday of their life
are not Really facing life reality.

There is no issue in our culture that has been more
Miss understood on all sides than sexual relations.

But when I come home from work, she makes me feel
so unappreciated.

A big part of growing up is learning to forgive.

The Author's personal note

For more than twenty-five years, in my ministry I have worked with couples who have experienced trouble in their marriage or relationship. There are times when the work can be discouraging and heartbreaking. Often the partners are angry, disillusioned, and in pain. Some feel betrayed by their mate, and love itself. They can't understand how their love has turned to pain and discouragement.

But in order for anyone to heal their relationship, there is much to learn, even about themselves and about relationships. But sadly, often they are overwhelmed by their day-to-day conflicts of an unbalance and distance in the relationship. Some may find that it is too late, and too hard, no matter how badly they truly want to make it work.

Although I am a pastor and pastoral counselor, I have experienced the emotional pain of break-up. But I now recognize that the ingredients of lasting love somehow remain to us in our human coming together a mystery, but in its understanding somehow should be understood. The devastation over the failure of my marriage led me to the writing of this book, *Yearning For Intimacy and Fulfillment: Compassionate and Emotional Needs* with a deeper purpose of a relationship. My decision to write about relationships represents a heartfelt conviction that there is no endeavor more worthy, no element of happiness more pivotal, and no process of intimacy and fulfillment more misunderstood than the process of love.

Our growing inability in this society to relate to one another in lasting loving relationships is reaching frightening proportions. Meaningless premarital sexual promiscuity is accepted as the norm. In our communities soon and very soon the two-parent family will be considered the exception. I recall years ago just before I was married my pastor (Eld. E McDowell) telling me, "Son the very measure of a good marriage should be in how much it encourages optimal intellectual, emotional and spiritual growth. We are right to want and need someone in our lives in order to seek wholeness." Our mate must become, and must remain, our most important source of affirmation and worth within our union, after ourselves.

ACKNOWLEDGMENT

When I started writing this book, I had no idea of the work that lay ahead. Had it not been for God, my family and friends, I couldn't have done it.

I give thanks to God for the opportunity He has given me to make a difference in this world in a more positive way by the life I live. I thank Him for the wisdom, simple, but effective He has given me to present this book to the readers.

I want to especially thank my children, for their strong support and encouragement that continues to surround me on my journey as an author, teacher, pastor, and father. My sons: Maurice, Donovan, Benjamin and Caleb. You are a great inspiration to me. Thanks to you, my most lovely and beautiful daughters, Laketta, Sheila and Quantil. It gives me so much joy in being your father; I love you all so much. Thanks to my beautiful daughters-in-law, Kelly and Melody, and my wonderful son-in-law Jason. I love you all so dearly. To my grandchildren, I "pop" love you very much.

Special love and thanks to my brothers, Jay, Will and Ben. Thanks to my lovely sisters, Deal and Helen. I give thanks to my wonderful sisters-in-law Carolyn and Glory. I also must say special thanks and love to all my terrific nieces and nephews, I am so proud of each you. Thanks for your warmth, love and appreciation of what I do.

I want to especially thank my wife and life partner, Linda, who read most of the revisions and gave me very good suggestions on how I might rearrange things or make them clearer. Your insightful suggestions from a female perspective have been necessary for my understanding and ability to bring this project to a close. Thanks once again for your continued support and patience with me while working on this project.

As a family, we are a part of this human creation of God; but we must always keep in mind that, as a family we all need the love and support of each other. I truly thank God for each and every one of you, and I love you all so dearly.

ACKNOWLEDGMENT # 2 —————————

This is a book that had to be written. For a few years now, I have been stirred by its calling long before my first book; *"An Accessible Approach to Obtain Wholeness."* But I realize that this second book may never have been written without the encouragement of my daughter, Laketta. Thanks for all your many calls, **"Pops have you started on that book yet?" "When are you going to get started? I will be done with my book before you will."** I love you baby-girl.

How can I thank you Kelly, My dear daughter-in-law. Thank you for your honest critique and criticism, which challenges me to do my best in the writing of this book. Special thanks to you for not only having the capability to straighten out my twisted sentences, but more importantly for challenging my concepts. Mostly needed when I had strayed too far off point and was unable to convey my meaning with proper grammar and punctuation. Your insightful suggestions and comments have provided an important and necessary balance.

Both of you have played a special part in making the writing of this book what it is. And it is your guidance that has made this project possible. The information relayed in these pages will allow people to grow and make their relationships better.

Chapter 1

An Assignment to Harass the Marriage in Christ by the Messenger of Satan

"For this reason a man shall leave his father and mother and be joined to his wife, and the two shall become one flesh." Eph.5: 31. (kjv.) The union of husband and wife merges two persons in such a way that little can affect one without also affecting the other. Oneness in marriage does not mean losing your personality in the personality of the other. Instead, it means caring for your spouse as you care for yourself, learning to anticipate his or her needs, helping the other person to become all that he or she can be. In Genesis 2: 24, it tells us God's plan for husband and wife to be one.

When a couple is in a conformity marriage they are in one of the greatest adventures sanctioned by God that is possible. When any couple has built a loving committed relationship and embark upon this adventure together in marriage, they will soon discover that they need to stay anchored in the strength of the Lord. Satan has gone all out to destroy the institution of marriage and its Biblical foundation for which it stand. Satan is going to attack you in every area of

promise in the vows that you made before God and man, and to each other.

This chapter is not written as a discussion to put fear in you concerning your marriage, but to alert you to be prayerful and watchful. Your marriage is going to be tested as it is with any couple. You will experience the ups and downs of married life, and in this life there will be some rain as well as some sunshine. The question is; do you really mean what you said in your marital vows? Marriage vows are, and should be required as the foundation of a successful marriage and the establishment of a happy and enduring home. Without these vows there can be no real marriage in the home, which you will endeavor to establish. Without them there will only be a vain effort. You are to live with tender love, care and consideration of each other. You are to conduct your lives in honesty and truth each day and your marriage will last.

For the Bible tells us in 1 Peter 5: 8 *"Be sober, be vigilant; because your adversary the devil, as a roaring lion, walketh about, seeking whom he may devour"* (kjv.) God's word tells us that Satan is both a liar and the father of lies and the truth is not in him. (2 Thess. 2:9, 10. Rev. 12:9, John 8:44.) Satan tries to deceive you into believing that he is all-powerful but the truth is his power is limited to his deception. The victory over the works of Satan is available to the believers of Christ. He gives us the key to freedom from all kinds of bondage and attacks of the enemy. In John 8:31,32 . . . If ye continue in my word, then are ye my disciples indeed; And ye shall know the truth, and the truth shall make you free.

The messenger of Satan comes against your union in many ways to harass you financially, spiritually, emotionally and even physically. But God's grace is sufficient to deliver you. Yes, God furnishes us the ability to stand against these diverse temptations of the enemy, but you as a union if at all possible must exercise your authority over the messengers of Satan. So many couples are harassed with all kinds of problems, and as long as they allow it to happen, Satan will bring all kinds of bad and damaging situations their way. But if they know the truth and act on what they know in faith by the authority that is within them, their marriage, and the relationship can be delivered from those attacks.

You may be experiencing some turbulent circumstances in your relationship at this moment that is causing you irritation and unrest. You may find yourself in a questionable situation not knowing what to do. What you must be firm on is that you not allow the fear of the enemy to make decisions for you. Here is what the word of the Lord says; "Trust in the Lord with all thine heart; and lean not unto thine own understanding. In all thy ways acknowledge Him, and He shall direct thy paths." Prov. 3:5,6. (kjv.)You may have to decree some things in faith in order to be able to see your way through your situation. Then the Lord will direct you.

So many of our relationships and marriages have been and are being devoured by the messengers of Satan, because we are not spiritually prepared to fight against the wiles of the Devil, nor are we prayerful and watchful as we have been warned to do so by the word of God. We are not fighting in a fleshly battle against Satan but we are in a spiritual warfare. Therefore the word tells us; "the weapons of our warfare are

not carnal, but mighty through God to the pulling down of strong holds." 2Cor.10: 4.

It is important for you to know and understand the advantage you have as a couple against the works of Satan. There will be various trials in a marriage but when committed to a loving and lasting relationship as a union being convinced that nothing shall move you and allowing patience to perfect you there will be victory over the works of Satan. When you unite as a couple in your fight, the power of Satan is weakened, and each time you dismiss a demon from his assignment and authority over your situation a great victory is won.

You may already know (if not "keep living") life will present some challenging situations from time to time, no marriage is exempt from them. Not one is excluded from some form of trouble. These troubles sometime come with advance warnings. You watch the development of these storm clouds but are unable to turn them back. Then there are those troubles that have no warning at all, seemingly out of a cloudless sky tragedy strikes your marriage. Although the effects of these troubles may be hard for you to bear, you must resolve within yourselves to stand firm in your belief when life's ills are trying to make you bitter and hopeless even against your spouse and others.

I am convinced that we will not live in this world without having some kind of problems. We will have some pains in this life and the life of our marriage; we will experience some disappointments, we will come to know the pressures of life. And we will have the joy-time to recover from one kind of setback or another. But regardless of any and all

these things, we are to be reassured that in spite of these things no matter how traumatizing it may be, we don't have to cumber and be destroyed by these things. With the two of you standing together speaking over your situation, you can make it!

Jesus did not tell us that we would have sunshine without some rain. Some people expect their marriage to be free of any problems in life, but of course they are always disappointed because in each life some rain must fall. In the mist of all of that, if we can look beyond each situation and realize that we have God on our side and we can make it, and if we can see that the Lord, who is bigger than any problem we may have, is with us, then we can make it thru any situation that comes to challenge our union. That old enemy who comes to torment God's people will try to bring every kind of troublesome situation into your marriage to defeat your commitment and the vows you made to each other. If you allow him, he will convince you that your marriage will not work, but through God, you have the power and authority to turn those Satanic lies back to the pits of Hell from which they came.

There is an enemy that fights against the people of God as well as in marriages; he comes only to bring you discouragement. Discouragement is something that will touch each and everyone's life at one time or another. But you cannot allow yourselves to be devastated by that, you must lift your heads and behold the Lamb of God who takes away the sins of the world, and realize that He is able to deliver you and bring you and your marriage out of your troubles with joy.

We are living in difficult times now; never before have we witnessed such uncertainties in relationships, the Satanic attack on marriages, communities, and families as we are in today's times. Never before have we witnessed so many families who are being put out of their homes in record numbers. They are no longer able to keep up with the high cost of their mortgage. And in today's economy even churches, large and small are going under bankruptcy protection facing foreclosures. The enemy is attacking what was once the base foundation of family.

We must be steadfast in the word of God, that in all these things, nothing shall be able to separate us from the love of God. If you stay with God and keep your marriage in His hands, in spite of the circumstances that you may be experiencing or those things that are about to come your way, He will stay with you and if God be for you, who or what can be against you?

God can give you not only another house but also a better house; God can restore your finances. People are losing their jobs in record numbers, many of whom are the sole provider for their household, but if you lose that one, God has a better job for you. Our God who is able to do all things, will restore all that is lost. So many relationships and marriages are in trouble but you must see the difference God can make in your lives. The circumstances and troubles you encounter by standing together will make you stronger, I remember back when I was a little kid I would often hear my mother say; "These things that come to test me are only the circumstances of life, what doesn't destroy me will only make me better."

You see, I learned a long time ago if you put your trust in the Lord, you can rise above your circumstances and not only that, you don't have to let your circumstances determine your outcome. Just a few years ago some friends of mine, who I will call Robert and Suzan, had just bought a very nice home, they both were working and had good jobs. They are a wonderful, loving couple who love each other very much, but as with any couple their commitment and faithfulness to each other was tested. Just a little more than two years ago, Robert's wife had taken ill. She was hit with a lingering disease and a heart attack. **(I am presenting this couple's experience hopefully to encourage you, because so many abandon their spouse in time of circumstances such as this.)** Robert and Suzan were in one of those "living deaths" or "what if in life" moment. They had worked hard to get to the place where they were. But due to the lingering disease, organ transplant and rehabilitation period and not having adequate insurance, they were experiencing a financial storm along with everything else. Robert and Suzan became one of the statistics that we all have known or heard of. There are hundreds of stories of people who are in financial bankruptcy, due to unseen financial expenses.

Because of the out of pocket expense that was being taken away from their everyday living and if that was not bad enough Robert lost his job, causing their financial storm to get even worse. Now both spouses were out of work and they had to move out of their home and lost one of their cars. They were in a financial mess, and it seemed like Suzan who was attacked with a storm of sickness was not getting any better. The probability of this loving couple coming out of such a storm seemed hopeless.

But this couple had a very strong love for each other. They both lost their jobs, home, and one of two cars and all of their finances went to medical bills. Suzan asked her husband: "Why suffer your life away with me? Please! Put me in a rest home and let them care for me I am not going to recover from this illness but you do have a chance to start over." Robert said to his wife: "God knows that I love you very much, and we will recover all together, I am not going anywhere, this will pass." Not long afterward Suzan's health was restored, she fully recovered from all of her sickness and is now back at work with a promotion. Robert has a better job with better pay, and they are doing just fine. It is paramount that the husband and wife be there for each, it should be a bond that not even the Devil from Hell (with all his tricks) should be able to break.

In the Bible there is some encouraging reading in the book of James 1:2-4, "*2 Consider it pure joy, my brothers and sisters, [a] whenever you face trials of many kinds, 3 because you know that the testing of your faith produces perseverance. 4 Let perseverance finish its work so that you may be mature and complete, not lacking anything.* (lab.) James did not say *if* you face trials, but *when* you face trials. He assumes that we will have trials and that it is possible to profit from them. The point here is not to pretend to be happy to face your trials, but we are to have a positive outlook.

The enemy is out to trouble you, that is his job, it does not matter who you are, whether you are rich or poor, whether you are young or old the works of the Devil have no respect of person. At one time or another you are going to be touched by something that is not pleasant. The Lord came to bring us peace but we must understand the enemy came to bring us trouble; he will trouble your marriage through dramatic setbacks and uncertainties, physically, financially and vocationally. But when you stand together in union, the Lord will be in your midst, and you will triumph in victory.

The possibilities for deepening the shared identity between you and your mate, however, are greatly heightened under duress provided there was already a strong attachment. Those feelings may have been overshadowed by the petty vicissitudes of daily life, but when a crisis hits, when there is a wellspring of your faith and trust that you can tap into, to defeat the enemy together you can produce moments of the deepest soul connection.

A loving and caring soul mate is uniquely suited to understand the emanations and emotional hurt and pain of his or her mate's cry. Even though the Lord may allow troubles for a reason beyond our understanding, the strength of a good and healthy relationship is a man and woman of faith, patience and endurance. This is the gift of a truly good marriage or long-standing relationship.

When a crisis hits, look at the victory the both of you have when you say "amen." By the authority you speak in faith against the evil works of Satan . . . you speak total recovery in your relationship and declare other things be restored in your relationship. Don't give up on your union through fear; what God had joined together let no man put asunder; keep walking in the light of His glory in unanimous authority Together the both of you can triumph in authority over the messengers of Satan The marriage in Christ can speak against the personal and marriage attacks that come against you and to proclaim victory.

I have had many battles and difficult situations but as I stay focused with my trust in God, I have triumphed each time. God will not put more on you than you can bear so be encouraged; your breakthrough is in your praise and worship. You have the power and authority in your hands as a union to keep your marriage, as God would have you to do; it is in your hands! There is this principle I have that keeps me focused, which is this: "The conduct of my faith and trust is governed by the principles in which I believe. These principles do not permit alteration of course in my faith."

Sometimes in the mist of our trials and troubles that we experience in our marriage, we find ourselves crying out through our prayers to God to help us. But even in the mist of that, we are careful not to allow Satan the deceiver to mislead us into thinking that we are all alone in the disturbances we may be experiencing. The Lord is a very present help in time of trouble His ears are open to our cry.

In the time of crisis don't doubt the power and authority of God. As a believable in God, you have the authority over the limited works of Satan, he cannot exceed his limit. But please be aware of the negative works of doubt as you trust God for a healthy marriage, doubt will drain the energy of your faith and trust in God. Doubt will deplete the resources of your patience. Patience gives us the experience and through experience we obtain hope.

The Bible reads like this in the second Chapter of Job; "Then the Lord said to Satan, have you considered my servant

Job? There is no one on earth like him; he is blameless and upright, a man who fears God and shuns evil. And he shall maintain his integrity, though you incited me against him to ruin him without any reason." Job 2:3. (lab). For any building, the foundation is critical. It must be deep enough and solid enough to withstand the weight of the building and other stresses. And our lives are like buildings, and the quality of our foundation will determine the quality of our life as a whole. Too often inferior materials are used, and when tests come, our lives crumble.

Job was tested. He was a wealthy and upright man. His life was filled with prestige, possessions, and people. Job lost all his possessions, his children, and his health. Suddenly his life was stripped down to his foundation and he was devastated. But the foundation of Job's life was built on God, therefore Job endured.

Through no fault of his own, Job lost wealth, children, and health. Even his friends were convinced that Job had brought this suffering upon himself. For Job, the greatest trial was not so much the pain of loss as it was not being able to understand why God allowed him to as He did. Those who love God are not exempt from trouble. Although we may not be able to understand fully the pain we experience, it can lead us to rediscover God.

Satan attempted to drive a wedge between Job and God by getting Job to believe that God was neither good nor just. Satan's powers are limited to what God allows, Satan had to ask God for permission to attack Job's wealth, children, and his health. God will not allow anymore on us that we can bear.

We must learn to recognize and not fear Satan's attacks on our marriages because Satan cannot exceed the limits that God sets. Don't let any troubles you experience in your marriage drive a wedge between you, your mate and God. Although you can't control how Satan may attack your union, you can always choose how you will respond when it does happen.

Through Job's suffering he learned that when nothing else was left, he had God, and that was enough. Through suffering, we learn that God is enough for our lives, marriage, and our future. We must love God regardless of whether He allows blessings or suffering to come to us. Trusting can be difficult when you are having trouble in your marriage, but the result of our trusting can turn things around for you, and often brings a deeper relationship with God and happiness in your marriage.

Job was a model of trust and obedience too, yet God permitted Satan to attack him in an especially harsh manner. Although the Lord loves us, believing and obeying Him does not shelter us from life's calamities, setbacks, tragedies, and sorrows. These troubles strike in all marriages, Christian and non-Christian alike. Even though we may not understand the difficulties we face sometimes, we must trust God as we show our faith to the world.

God is all wise and all-powerful. His will is perfect, yet He doesn't always act in ways that we understand. When Job was at his point of despair, God spoke to him, showing him His great power and wisdom. Job showed the kind of trust that we should have. When everything is stripped away, we should recognize that God is there with us to help us. He is not insensitive to our suffering. God is present, His ears are open to our cry; whatever issues you may experience in your marriage, know that God is sufficient and able to help us in time of crisis.

CHAPTER 2
BEDROOM BOREDOM!! WHAT?

Defraud ye not one the other, except it be with consent for a time, that ye may give yourselves to fasting and prayer; and come together again, that Satan temp you not for your incontinency. (1Cor. 7:5.)

The husband should give his wife what is due her as his wife, and the wife should be as fair to her husband. The wife has no longer full rights over her own person, but share it with her husband. In the same way the husband shares his personal rights with his wife. They do not cheat each other of normal sexual intercourse, unless of course you both decide to abstain temporarily to make special opportunity for prayer and fasting. But afterwards you should resume relations as before, or you will expose yourselves to the obvious temptation of Satan (1 Corinthians 7:3-8). A friend of mine whom I have known for many years, was in a meeting with me and a few other pastors and we ended up talking on the subject of incontinency. He said "When passion burns within you, you should remember that it was given to you for good purposes." I would like to add to this statement by saying that we should also be aware at all times that Satan the tempter, is someplace nearby waiting to tempt us in our incontinency.

Sexual temptations are difficult to withstand because they are normal and natural desires that God has given us. One of the purposes of sexual intercourse is that children may be born to the new union and become a delight to the parents. Now God could have accomplished this purpose by having a couple spit into a common receptacle. The female could then drink the contents and become pregnant. But His infinite mind conceived the idea of sex, the union between male and female that brings more physical pleasure than any other activity. Whether sex fulfills a desire to have children, satisfies the sex drive, reassures one another of love, or relaxes the nervous system, it all adds up to providing the most exciting physical experience known to humans. God created sex for our pleasure, and He wants us to delight in it. Sex is an enjoyable experience for married couples.

Marriage is God's way of satisfying these natural sexual desires and to strengthen married couples against temptation. In this union married couples have the responsibility to love and care for each other; therefore, husbands and wives should not withhold themselves sexually from one another, but should fulfill each other's needs and desires in a loving, caring and responsible way.

But in reality what I call "bedroom boredom" it is the "sexually unfulfilled" state of being in marriages. Particularly women, those who are in so many marriages that speaks of being sexually unfulfilled and passionately suffering from the need of intimacy in their relationship. Therefore due to lack of knowledge or un-willingness in consideration to render satisfactory pleasure to our spouses, this misunderstanding can cause intensifying sexually frustration with our spouses.

God does not intend faithfulness in marriage to be boring, lifeless, pleasureless, and dull. Sex is a gift God gives to married people for their mutual enjoyment. Real happiness comes when we decide to find pleasure in the relationship God has given or will give us and to commit ourselves to making sexual intercourse pleasurable for our spouse. The real danger is in doubting that God knows and cares for us. We then may resent His will and carelessly pursue sexual pleasure without His blessing.

In my work as a pastor and pastoral counseling for more than twenty years, I take joy in making full proof of my ministry and calling. During this time I have been blessed to be the pastor of several churches. And as a pastor, I have always considered pastoral counseling to be an integral part of my ministry. As a clergyman and spiritual guide of the word based on my years of experience in the field of ministry, I have come to realize that Biblical counseling is a needful part of the whole. I stand on the fact that in Biblical counseling when the love of God is ministered in a balance of mercy and truth it provides both a supportive environment and direction for understanding even in spousal relationships. Therefore for the sake of incontinency I seek to give some material of understanding to this very important subject matter.

The enjoyment of sex in marriage is appropriate and should be pleasurable. God gave us our sex drives not to make us miserable but to bring us fulfillment in relationships. God is the creator of sex, and He was pleased with all that He had made including our human sexuality. The sexual act is not just for making babies but is also intended for pleasure between a husband and wife. It is appropriate and right that the husband and wife give pleasure to each other through intimacy and intercourse. It is a blessing from God.

It is also the will of God that sex be an intimate communication tool. Sexual touching is a form of communication that uses the body to express love from the spirit, emotion, mind, and will. God created us as sexual creatures with sex drives and feelings. He intended that sexual intimacy for the committed relationship of married couples. Sexual union in marriage is provided by God for couples to experience complete closeness and that they are to be united and to be "one flesh." And said, "For this cause shall a man leave father and mother, and shall cleave to his wife: and they twain shall be one flesh? Wherefore they are no more twain, but one flesh. What God hath joined together, let not man put asunder." (Matt.19:56. kjv).

Our attitude toward sexuality and sensuality should have a lasting influence on the pleasure we derive from and the joy we bestow upon one another in our marriage. It should be the most intimate and private of human acts, as we reveal ourselves to each other, and as we give ourselves to each other, we join our excited bodies and soaring spirits our lives and our being, in passion and joy. In the bed, today and through a thousand tomorrows, our willingness to serve, pleasure, nurture, and heal each other, should be now and forever. There is no deeper communication between two people than the act of intercourse between two committed lovers through their marriage.

Upon my arrival to church early one Saturday morning to meet with my first appointment with an older couple for a counseling session, I was pleased to see that they had just arrived as I was pulling into the driveway. For the protection of their identity, let's just call them brother Joe and sister Betty. This couple was in their early to mid 70s. As we all were getting out of our cars about the same time we greeted each other in the manner as we often do and entered into the church. While we were walking down the hall to my office, I noticed how happy the two were. I said to myself "I wonder what in the world could these two need counseling for." It seemed like they were so very happy together. This is the kind of success you would like to see after each counseling session.

As we entered into my office I asked them to please have seat. After they were seated I said to them, "Brother Joe and sister Betty it is so good and refreshing to see you here this morning! Please let us have prayer before we start." After prayer I asked them "Now how can I be of help to such a fine couple as you? Tell me, what brings you here today? The both of you really look so nice together. Who would like to begin first?" I noticed that neither of them was eager to start, so I said to them, "I have my notes here with me from your phone call and you said it had something to do with the bedroom? Now this will be a very good place to start." Being an older couple (to help them feel more comforted) I said to them "Maybe it would help by telling me what problems you are having in the bedroom?"

Brother Joe begin to talk, "Well, Elder Johnson I am glad you are willing to talk to us about this, I didn't know that you would be willing to talk with us about anything like this. You see, sometimes we are ready at different times, when I am ready she is not and sometimes when she is ready I am not or too tired. We both like being together very much and we enjoy being with each other." I said to them, "Brother Joe, sister Betty you don't have a problem." They both responded at the same time "We don't?" Sister Betty responded afterward, "Then what is the matter?" I replied, "there is no problem, you both enjoy being together and expressing your love to each in the most intimate way, this is all good."

In the way of humor, I said to them "there are just those moments when one of you is asleep and the other one is not, rest and enjoy yourself. Try slowing it down and set the mood with more passion that you both can feel good and get ready for that moment. Enjoy doing some kissing, along with some foreplay, rubbing and feeling sensitive parts of each other's body, building up to the moment. This way you are also allowing each other to get ready for that moment of love and intimacy and communicate to learn the needs of each other. So, take your time and enjoy each other as you always have." I gave them a few other techniques on celebrating their relationship and just before we had payer to end our session, brother Joe said to me, "Elder Johnson, Betty and I feel so much better now! Thank you very much." Sister Betty then replied, "Elder, I sure didn't know you talk like that, you are some pastor!"

After our session was over this couple left my office feeling much better about themselves and no one was made to feel embarrassed, and that I was well pleased with. Two weeks later brother Joe stops by my office and said to me, "Elder

Johnson! All is well at home with Betty and me; we are just doing fine, thank you sir."

Loving relationships demand expression. Caring will be communicated. We express who we are and how we feel through the only instruments available to us, our bodies. Our bodies include minds that think, senses that feel, skin and limbs that touch, and genitals that perform a variety of functions and respond to stimuli. We are, "embodied," and our "bodies are always sexual bodies." Sex and sexuality are therefore central to our consideration of what is involved in being in a relationship through love and marriage.

Perhaps the most important point to emphasize, however, is that sexual experience between male and female is a good thing. This pleasurable, fulfilling experience is appropriate and pleasing in the eyes of God. These words are expressed in romantic poetry, which some actually find difficult to accept as belonging in the Bible:

> How fair and pleasant you are,
> O loved one, delectable maiden!
> You are stately as a palm tree,
> And your breasts are like its clusters.
> I say I will climb the palm tree
> And lay hold on its branches.
> Oh, may your breasts be like clusters of the vine,
> And the scent of your breath like apples,
> And your kisses like the best wine
> That goes down smoothly, gliding over lips and teeth.
> I am my beloved's

> And his desire is for me.
> Come, my beloved,
> Let us go forth into the fields,
> And lodge in the villages;
> Let us go early to the vineyards,
> And see whether the vines have duded,
> And whether the grape blossoms have opened
> And the pomegranates are in bloom.
> There I will give you my love.

This most delightful verse in found in the Bible in the "Song of Solomon"7:6-12. In that book it has a number of passages like this, rich in detail of sensual and romantic pleasure.

I move to disagree with those writers who idealize wild, simultaneous orgasm; I believe that in some ways they do a disservice. Couples might read these descriptions and question their own sex life. "Something's wrong with us; we're falling short." Chasing after and never achieving some magic orgasm that involves a reaction roughly equivalent to a nuclear explosion can make you feel inferior and inhibit your sexual enjoyment. Sexual intercourse is a form of human expression, and like conversation it can be animated or subdued, profound or frivolous, dramatic or matter-of-fact. If it suits your mood, it will be highly satisfying. Any couple with positive attitudes toward sex and consideration for enhancing their mutual pleasure will soon discover the various responses and positions that are most satisfying to them at different times, under different circumstances. If the purpose of the human expression of love is served, any form that the expression takes is good and wholesome.

Husband and wife should find happiness and loving pleasure in each other; you should never be so preoccupied in self and other things that you have no "fulfillment" time to love and enjoy the one whom you are married to. *"Ministers are not excluded;"* I have given a series of such counseling sessions with pastors and minister's wives who are sexually frustrated. Their main concerns are; "My husband is so preoccupied with others' concerns and being a preacher that I don't know what it feels like anymore to be romanced and sexually fulfilled. When we do have what he calls sex, to me it is a boring routine, he acts like this is something he had to do just to keep our marriage together. Pastor Johnson, Where is the love in this? Where is the romance? Where is the passion? Where is the stimulation in love making?"

This is the cry of frustration of so many "first ladies" today they feel neglected and left out in the relationship. There was one couple in one of my sessions who was having problems and his wife said "When I told my husband that sometimes I need to be sexually stimulated, and asked him if we could take time and have foreplay, he acted like I said a bad word and he tried to make me feel ashamed just for expressing my desire."

One of the greatest barriers to happiness in marriages is self-preoccupation. People get so preoccupied with their own little world they live in a world of one. That's "narcissism." My definition of a narcissistic person is someone who is having a great big love affair with himself but can't stand the object of his affections. That can be a problem. Until a person is able to break out of that, through unconditional love that awaits him by his mate, he will stay very much alone and feel very strange. The thing that triggers self-preoccupation is self-importance.

I believe that one of the laws of maturity is to love yourself, to accept yourself, and to forget about yourself. To love yourself means to accept yourself exactly as you are because that's how God created you and that's the way He wants you. To accept yourself means you are never going to be anybody else because when you (mimic) imitate others you're going to copy the wrong things. To forget about yourself means you really are not that important, there are two in this marriage, so get on with the business of intimacy, the enjoyment of each other and lovemaking.

OPEN DISCUSSION IS ESSENTIAL.

Communication is so important between couples concerning their sexual relationship. Couples should discuss their love-making, both in bed and also when there are far away from the passion of the moment. You should express your feelings, preference, thoughts and problems. But you should be gentle with each other, for each of you invests a great deal of yourself and your egos in your sexual relationship. Any criticism can be quite hurtful, because when your beloved discloses failings of sexuality, a deep trust is being displayed. There is nothing wrong with a little positive reinforcement whether it is a raised eyebrow, a little shared joke, or a few words of satisfaction or appreciation.

When eager, trusting, and sensitive to each other's needs and demands, the couples can experience the wonder of love as it overflows into new emotions and experiences. Together they are capable of deep physical and emotional response and involvement. Neither should be startled by the fervor or the timidity of the other's approach; nor by the intensity of your own or your partner's response; or even by the changing roles that each of you will assume at different times in love-making.

As your sexual life continues and patterns of arousal are established and as you learn what pleases and turns the other on, repetition of familiar patterns of sexual arousal will be comfortable and exciting. Variety, on the other hand, is just as, if not more, exciting and keeps your sexual relationship stimulating and rewarding. Lovemaking that is too patterned and rigid can make sexual relations dull and burdensome.

Lovemaking between husband and wife never needs to be boring or routine. God created us with a desire, which is much like taking a long, cold drink of water on a hot summer afternoon. "Let your fountain be blessed, and rejoice in the wife of your youth. As a loving hind and a graceful doe, let her breasts satisfy you at all times; be exhilarated always with her love" (proverbs 5:18-19).

Our God is a creative God. He can give us creative ideas in our sex lives. Do you ever pray for creativity from God in this area? Well you should. Do you ever pray that you may be a blessing to your mate in your physical relationship? You should. Do you ask the Lord for His point of view when you experience hang-ups from your childhood? You may. The Lord is interested in all our problems including those we may have in this area.

One Old Testament word for intercourse is to *know*. "Adam *knew* Eve his wife, and she conceived" (Genesis 4:1, 25 kjv). This is a beautiful word because I believe sex is total communication-body, soul, and spirit. Total knowledge completes communication. And that is what it should be, but it is often not. More likely one of the first things a marriage couple should do is to know and understand the facts. Many people have a terrible time speaking out loud the correct name for parts of the body. Then they wonder why it is difficult for them to communicate about sex.

Over the years I have come to believe that there is also another reason why God created our sexual identities in marriage. It is to illustrate the value of self-giving and of sacrificial love. You see, sexual expression is the most satisfying when we give pleasure to one anther in marriage. We are created by the Lord as sexual human beings to instruct us about Himself and the purpose of our sexuality, that we were created to be in relationship and that we are incomplete in ourselves and need each other to experience completeness. I would dare to believe that sex by itself would be little more than animal appetite. I believe that in a marriage, genuine love combines sexual desire with all the other components that build the highest kind of relationship between husband and wife. Love is devotion in marriage, friendship, tenderness, self-control, kindness, and loyalty blended with desire in an intimate relationship with your spouse.

If one would really admit to the fact, you would agree that the sexual urge, separated from the other true aspects of a relationship; selfish desires to dominate, conquer, force, or surrender, is animal. But genuine love idealizes, controls, and conforms sexual desire to true living. Love is other-person-centered. Sex without love is self-centered, a craving for physical satisfaction, physical release. True committed love, on the other hand, is the affectionate concern that craves an intimate sharing with ones soul mate.

In my years of working in ministry with pastoral counseling being an integral part of that ministry, I find it to be a common fear among married couples to have an intimate discussion concerning their sexual relationship. When having a discussion about money problems or that the bills are too high, words seem to come so easily. Words also come freely in a discussion with your spouse concerning other marital problems the couple may be experiencing.

Open dialogue with your partner is the key to knowing, to penetrating the mystery of the other who is different from you. Couples must talk about sex and express exactly what they want, what they like and dislike. This dialogue serves a dual purpose: It expresses your needs and desires, and it allows and requires you to consider the needs and desires of the other. Sexual talk is itself erotic, and it breeds intimacy. As mentioned earlier, dialogue assumes equality; it requires recognition of and respect for the other's idiosyncratic sexual feelings and preferences.

What it boils down to is safe sex, sex that is truly consensual. No one should engage in sex that is not mutually pleasurable. We have to learn to say no to sex that feels like conquest or submission in the wrong way. Sex that expresses hostility or anger, or that is manipulative is wrong. Sex can transform the ordinary reaching far beyond the mere meeting of two bodies, but also a pleasurable release of tension. It is a graceful experience each time couples mate with each other in the most fervent, erotic way. The greater the pleasure that men and women give to each other in bed and in every other dimension of their relationship, the more God is present in that union. The act of our sexuality can fuel the spiritual core of our relationship.

What seems to be the most difficult between the husband and wife is to have a very intimate conversation concerning any sexual struggles that may exist in their relationship. It appears to be even more difficult for the husband than it is for the wife. As men, we tie our masculinity to our sexual ability, so we find it difficult to discuss sexual problems. It hits us where it hurts-our manhood. We want our sexual relationship to work without any hassles of talking about it. To have a discussion about it just feels weird. One may even feel a bit strange or awkward talking to his spouse concerning any sexual struggles that may exist in their relationship.

Open communication, when done prayerfully and in consideration of each other's feelings, is the only way to fully deal with sexual problems. Most women tend to value working through such problems, and do not relate masculinity to a man's sexual performance. For the most part, women are not afraid to talk about sexual problems, and it seems that they are not so highly concerned with sexual performance as men are. Her concern is that he put in enough time that they both come to full satisfaction. On the other hand, men tend to be performance-oriented. They regard any problem as their fault.

It is important to talk to your wife during your sexual act to make sure she is comfortable with and receiving pleasure from your actions. As difficult as it may be because of your masculinity, you need to ask her if what you're doing feels good to her. Just because it feels good to you, it doesn't mean it feels good to your wife. So find out what pleases your wife the most in foreplay and what brings her to orgasm.

As men we need to find out what our wife's needs are, and what she likes or dislikes about sex. Just because some of you men may have been married for years, it could be awkward for you ask, but you may discover that that same old thing you have been doing over, and over, and over is not giving her pleasure. There are a variety of ways as well as positions to make lovemaking more enjoyable and pleasurable. Choose the right time to talk about it, other than right before or after, which could be the worst time if things are not going well. So talk about your sex life to your mate but at a more comfortable time. To focus more on developing the relationship with your wife and through communication and listening, it will contribute to sex becoming a strong, healthy aspect of the relationship. Now I do not rule out quickies, they can be and are very enjoyable and exciting when done at the right place and in the right passionate moment they can excite pleasurable responses.

BIBLICAL COUNSELING SHOULD BE AN INTEGRAL PART OF MINISTRY

CONCERNING SEXUAL RELATIONSHIP

One Sunday afternoon after our church service had ended, I called for a meeting in my office with part of my church staff to have a discussion with them concerning an up-coming event to be held at the church the following week. During our meeting there came a knock at the door. One of my deacons opened the door and asked them to come in. It was one of the young ladies who work with the youth department of the church. As she entered she said "Pastor I am sorry to come into your meeting but my husband and I would like to be counseled by you this week." I said, "yes, how soon would you like to meet?" She answered, "Tomorrow please?" So I said, "that would be fine, can we meet at 10am?" She replied, "Yes pastor we will see you tomorrow." After the appointment date was set, my staff and I continued with the meeting.

On Monday morning upon my arrival to the church, I noticed the couple (to protect their identity, let's call them sister Jill and brother Jack) had also arrived. After getting out of my car I went into the church and as I entered into the hallway the couple was sitting there waiting. I greeted them with a big hello!! "My dear children how are you?" Sister Jill replied, "Hi pastor, you are late!" I said, "yes I am sorry, please forgive me it is five past ten AM. But the Lord has blessed me to arrive safely and I do thank Him. Now please come on into my office and let us have prayer so we may start the session."

After we had prayer I asked them "Now how may I help you? Who would like to go first?" Sister Jill said, "Yes pastor, I will go first. You see Jack and I have been married for two years now and we have three children. He is a good father to our children and a good husband to me. He has a good job and we have a nice home, a car and his truck." I said to them "you all are blessed and seem to be doing the right things in your marriage I am pleased, so what brings you here today?"

As Jack was sitting so quietly and waiting for his turn to speak, at the same time he appeared to be in fear that his masculinity was about to be crushed and pounded upon. Sister Jill continued, now in a somewhat low and shameful voice, "Pastor when Jack and I are in our bedroom in an intimate relationship most of the time he leaves me unfulfilled. He is full early and I am not, can you talk to us about that please?" I said "yes, I think so" and turned to her husband and said "but let us hear from brother Jack now" Then I asked him, "brother what light can you shed with us on this concern?" His wife replied, "Yes, I would like to hear what he has to say also." I said to her "It is your husband's time to speak now sister Jill, go on brother Jack, tell me just what you think the problem could be." "Well pastor, to be honest, it is kind of difficult to talk about this so I will say it this way. When we do what we do and I get through I am ready for bed but she is not. Sometimes she wants to keep going and it seems like all night." "Thank you brother Jack, now may I offer a few suggestions that I think will help the both of you?

"First of all brother, there is nothing wrong with either of you. You all have a full life together. May I suggest that neither of you get in a hurry? Sexual intercourse between a husband and wife is to be enjoyed; it is a celebration of their relationship, this is a blessing from God. Keep in mind that there is a difference in how you respond as a man, than in the way your wife does. A man can achieve an erection without much foreplay. And understand that the actual intercourse is a more emotional connection of the union.

Communicate; try to understand what gets your wife to full satisfaction. An important fact to know is that most women achieve orgasms more from clitoral stimulation than the actual intercourse. So you must take your time and learn what works for your mate and how to stimulate each other's bodies through what I call "romantic foreplay."

The bedroom is not the only place where you are to enjoy the fulfillment of your sexual intercourse, try another room in your house. Make date nights. Sometimes you should begin the night (or day) with some good communication. Chances of an enjoyable sexual experience increase. Don't always make it a rush job, see your sexual experience as involving the conversation, foreplay, intercourse, orgasm, and after play. And always keep in mind that your wife is made to enjoy a gentle, gradual process as part of her arousal for intercourse. You should try to make it less goal—oriented but a more pleasurable sexual encounter."

Before we ended our session with prayer, I shared the word of God with them concerning their union and gave them a few other techniques. The session ended on a good note. Before leaving my office, the couple was very happy that this meeting had taken place. I was pleased to see them that way, they were also in a big hurry to get home or find a nearby hotel.

As stated in this chapter, sex is God's gift to His creatures. It is He who has endorsed sex, but He has also restricted its expression to those committed to each other in marriage. And it is the will of God that it be motivated by love and commitment, not lust. It is for the couples' mutual pleasure and fulfillment, not selfish enjoyment.

I believe that one of the most explicit statements on sex in the Bible can be found in the Song of Songs. Its sensuous language has often been criticized through the centuries. The purity and sacredness of love represented in that book is greatly needed in our day where distorted attitudes about love and marriage are commonplace. And the point we tend to drive home is that God created sex and intimacy, and they are holy and good when enjoyed within the bounds of marriage. The union of a husband and wife honor God when they love and enjoy each other.

THE PHYSIOLOGY OF SEXUALITY

Genital sexual arousal is somewhat similar in males and females. The penis, the clitoris, and the labia contain sponge-like tissue. When sexual arousal occurs, blood is pumped forcefully and "locked" into the erectile tissue, causing the tissue to become extended and swollen (tumescent). Penile erection occurs in the male and clitoral erection in the female. The clitoris is the initial center of sexual arousal in the woman's body. Very gentle manipulation of the clitoris and labia during foreplay normally serves to heighten the woman's state of arousal and intensify her desire for penetration.

As sexual arousal increases, the labia become more firm and open wider to accept the penis. The penis enlarges and becomes very firm and erect, enabling it to enter into the vagina. While sexual stimulation causes an increase in vaginal secretions that lubricate the vaginal passage and makes it easier for the penis to penetrate, on occasion, however, lubrication may not extend to the labia or external genital area. At such time, the man or woman can use their

33

fingers to draw vaginal lubricating fluid toward the vaginal opening.

As arousal becomes intense, the entire nervous system becomes involved. Pressure on sensitive nerve endings in the genitals create the distinctive, mixed sensation of pleasure and discomfort characteristic of sexual arousal. The woman is psychologically prepared, open, and eager to receive the man; the man's whole being is concentrated and focused, ready to enter into and give himself to the woman.

When excitement is quite intense, and both partners feel ready, the man inserts his penis into the vagina. Both, the husband and wife may normally engage in a series of rhythmic, thrusting motions of the pelvis to increase the pleasurable contact and friction. These movements, which may last for a while, cause the physical and emotional excitement to build to a final "climax," at which moment nervous tension is released in orgasm. As the penis spurts seminal fluid into the vagina, the man experiences ejaculation and release of tension, which are his highest excitement and greatest physical pleasure in sex. In the woman, spasmodic contraction of the genital muscles and body may vary from highly spasmodic to almost imperceptible.

The orgasms of the male and female result in the relaxation of the genital blood vessels that maintain erection and tumescence; relief from genital congestions quickly follow. If stimulation is stopped short of orgasm, however, relief occurs very slowly. In some women, such relief may take an hour or more. The pattern of orgasm in the woman is more varied. She may experience different responses at different times. Some responses are quite marked and intense, with automatic muscular spasms in the pelvic regions; some are less intense and sometimes imperceptible. A woman's orgasm is not always so definite or localized as a man's. In some, it may be a more diffuse reaction of well-being, satisfaction, and intimate union.

Although a male may often reach orgasm quite soon after intromission, his ability to maintain an erection and prolong intercourse will increase with experience. This may mean that the female will often not reach orgasm at the same time the man does. Studies show that most women achieve orgasms from clitoral stimulation rather than actual intercourse. But any stimulation that she finds pleasurable and that helps her achieve orgasm is important to the culmination of sexual fulfillment for both husband and wife. With experience and communication, the couple learns the kind and amount of preliminary stimulation each requires in achieving deep physical and emotional satisfaction, fulfillment and release. As experience grows, the couple learns more about "timing" and will sometimes be able to reach orgasm more or less together.

PLEASURABLE SENSUALITY

Certain areas of the body are especially responsive to sexual stimulation. The mouth, the lips, the genital organs and the areas around them, and a woman's breasts are the primary areas that are sensitive and capable of arousing sexual feeling. People and moods vary, they are not all the same. For some, the ears, neck, shoulders, back, legs, etc. may also be quite sensitive. Stimulation of these areas of the body by rubbing, fondling, stroking, and kissing gradually will produce stronger physical and emotional arousal. Excitement and sexual tension increase.

In "foreplay," no areas of the body are forbidden, and there is no right or wrong. Whatever actions are desired and pleasurable for the couple are appropriate. A combination of passion, consideration, sensitivity and tenderness should accompany foreplay. Both the husband and wife should do all they can to stimulate and increase the partner's pleasure and excitement. For the male, whose body is stimulated quickly and intensely, it is not always easy to prolong lovemaking and foreplay. For the female, whose total pleasure may be greatly enhanced by prolonged physical intimacy, and whose body may respond to have sex more slowly, it is sometimes frustrating to have sexual activity quickly. A couple able to tell each other what their needs are, who can learn to respond to those needs and prolong love-making and sexual stimulation, can learn not to concentrate on achieving their individual orgasms but rather their shared pleasure.

The mutual tenderness, concern, thoughtfulness and physical closeness displayed in lovemaking proves much more assuring, supportive and meaningful than the act of intercourse itself. When a couple joins physically to fulfill their love, the concern each has for the other's physical pleasure and emotional fulfillment will enrich and enhance their own pleasure and fulfillment.

Overcoming early awkwardness and discovering how to please each other is an intimate experience that binds couples closely together. Beauty and excitement accompany first encounters in lovemaking, and there is something special about that first, tentative kiss which you will always remember. Lovemaking in marriage involves a dimension of art and skill that comes only with experience and sensitivity.

MOOD SETING

The psychological context in which intercourse takes place is important and can and should vary. Mood setting is good. The freedom to proceed in an unhurried manner can be pleasurable, and lovemaking does not have to be in the same old position or same place, a change is good. Romantic and seductive words provide a special aura that enhances a couple's pleasure. When the mood of the day has been warm and loving and you are feeling psychologically close, intercourse is also a celebration of your loving friendship.

We can contribute to the romance of lovemaking by looking and smelling good. Brush your teeth, take a shower, and men if your stubble hairs cause rash to your wife when kissing and rubbing your face to on hers, take a shave. Give your wife time to take a bath, which will often relax her and make the sexual encounter more pleasurable. And remember, slow down, lovemaking is not a rush job; sometime the couple should creates a sensational atmosphere for the pleasure and enjoyment of it. So don't be in a rush to "get it over with so you can go to sleep." Keep in mind your wife is made to enjoy a gentle, gradual process as part of her arousal for intercourse. And for most women the experience involves the conversation, foreplay, intercourse, orgasm, and after-play.

For these reasons as stated, most women need more preliminary sex play than men in order to achieve sexual satisfaction. It is also true that most of them do not realize how great an effort a man may have to make to delay his own reactions. But if the man can make the effort and if there is good communication between them so that they understand each other's needs and desires in this respect, he will find it worthwhile.

The husband should keep in mind in leading up to the moment, not only does the type of genital foreplay that a woman prefers vary from one woman to another, the same woman may have different preferences at different times. Open communication is essential to understanding your wife's needs. It is recognized and understood that many women enjoy firm, sustained rubbing of the shaft on the clitoris. While other women prefer clitoral stimulation alternated with caresses of the vaginal lips, the moms, or the mouth of the vagina; or gentle, teasing, stroking just outside the vaginal opening. When couples can indicate these preferences to each other, they will reach the place of mutuality in response more often than a couple tongue-tied by ignorance and shyness. There are wide individual differences in this matter, as stated by the wife of one of the couples I was counseling on this same subject matter. The wife stated; "I like it best of all, when my husband can get three or four of his fingers crammed inside of me while rubbing my clitoris." A couple's feelings about sex and their feelings about each other are the keys to success or failure in achieving mutual sexual satisfaction.

If a husband and wife do not have fun with each other in bed, they will have neither the motivation nor the courage to tackle the more complex problems in a personality conflict. When two people are trying to grow in their mutual lovemaking, a psychological tone develops in their relationship that greatly enhances their attractiveness to each other. Familiarity breeds contempt only for those who have stopped growing. For faithful lovers, it breeds both heightened pleasure and even heightened mystery. We must choose to make love happen. And our marriage is the place where we get the greatest chance to work at human love.

Lovemaking is good for the heart

Do you not know that men who have sex just twice a week have about half the risk of developing cardiovascular disease than those having sex once a month, according to a study in the American Journal of Cardiology? Sex lowers blood pressure and relieves stress, according to research found in the journal Biological Psychology. You will sleep better after having sex, Research shows the oxytocin released during orgasm promotes sleep. Even though sex is a form of exercise, it is also urgency that we understand it's true meaning and purpose. AU.K. Study found that having sex three times a week over the course of a year burns about the same number of calories as running 120 Kilometers (about 75 miles). Now, my brothers and sisters that certainly beats sweating in the gym.

We are in such a hurry these days to get to the fulfillment and satisfaction in lovemaking that we miss out on the pleasure and the enjoyment in getting there. Thereby sometime causing sexual forestation rather than sexual fulfillment and satisfaction. "Enjoy who you are with" be thankful for the person the Lord has put in your life to receive such love and pleasure from and for you to give such love and pleasure to.

CHAPTER 3
ATTITUDE ADJUSTMENT IN RELATIONSHIPS

As couples in relationships today, are we doing the requirements that are expected of us for personal growth and happiness? I must also ask the question, are we really listening to each other as well as ourselves? There is a great deal of negative sentiment in most relationships today about each gender. We should take a good look at the language we sometimes choose to use when we are communicating with our mate. We must understand that anytime we go from our promise to a negative attitude, there is now an unbalance and disturbance in the relationship.

We are at a point now that in so many of our "I do" relationships it seems like couples are not even friends anymore. They live in the same house or apartment and may not speak to each other for days, when words are spoken between them there are more negative words than there are positive ones. There is a problem, but what each needs to know is that when we come to the end of the day; respect, love and kindness are foundational elements that are needed in order for any of us to have a healthy, loving relationship.

Happiness is probably the most elusive emotion and the most difficult to define. It is probably one of the easiest emotions to feel. Happiness comes to us as a direct result of positive self-worth, personal attitudes, specific actions, and an essential principle in behavior connected to the way in which we relate to our mate and others. And one can say that happiness is the gratitude and appropriate behavior of us as human beings and how it fits into our life process.

There are similar interests in male and female. We all have similar desires. And it is best understood when we remove all the untrue characterizations, the ego, all the baggage and the hurt that fundamentally distance us. Both men and women want the same thing; a loving, healthy relationship. The most important thing for us to take a defining look at is how we as couples are relating to each other.

If our attitude toward our mate is negative, we are going to experience an unhappy world. There will always be too much traffic on the interstate, the service in the restaurant will always be too slow, our children's rooms will never be clean enough, the weather will never be nice enough, and we'll feel that family and friends should have done things better or differently. A positive attitude toward life, your mate as well as others is a requirement for a life of happiness. When negative situations do arise as they do in everyone's life, the ability to see problems as challenges presenting opportunities for creative solutions is the difference between failure and success, unhappiness and happiness.

The freedom to be who we are in a positive way, good feelings, respect of ourselves and our mate, satisfaction, contentment, peace of mind, joy, laughter, and happiness are the human rewards of life. They are available to all of us for the doing with the right attitude and in relationships, not for the demanding, asking or wishing. Our happiness comes to **us** as the direct result of positive self-worth, having fellowship with Christ, personal attitudes, specific actions and the way in which we relate to our mate and others.

Those who are fearful, distrustful, and dislike themselves will find it very difficult to freely love. It's simply because they cannot remove the focus from themselves. They have not discovered their own identity and ego strength. Because they are uncomfortable with themselves, they are preoccupied with themselves and use vast amounts of mental energy to protect their self-image. In an oversimplified way, such individuals are somewhat like the basketball player who notices that his shoelace is untied. His concentration is broken. He can't dribble, shoot, or fake; if someone steps on that shoelace, he will land on his face or the hardwood floor. He is completely unable to turn his attention outward.

Therefore, someone who is preoccupied with himself or herself through dislike of self will not be at peace with self. So often this frustration is taken out on your mate. Satan's desire is to destroy your relationship and deceive you into thinking that you have no problem at all, and if there is a problem it is always with your mate or someone else, not you. This causes you to harbor a spirit of deception imbedded in the disposition of selfishness, which will prevent you from socializing with your mate in a loveable

Christ like manner. Also those who have a lot of drama in their lives are allowing Satan to deceive them with a disagreeable disposition or attitude.

Satan's goal is to mislead you into wrong deeds, actions and thoughts. The price we pay when we allow ourselves to be misled by him is that he spiritually blinds you from the truth. Therefore you are permitting him the opportunity to deposit inside of you deadly emotions of ills and resentful feelings against your mate. We deserve to be happy. The happiness that flows from a loving relationship and the happiness that comes from a rewarding job are exciting to experience. Happy people often have both.

One of the greatest causes of unhappiness is self-pity. It can absolutely immobilize us from any action that may bring us happiness. There are many people who lose much needed sleep, crying day and night, about things that have happened in their lives that they can't change. To wallow in self-pity is to play the victim. Sometimes in relationships our mates will disappoint us. There may be those who may not love us the way we think they should, or events and plans don't work out as we expected them to. When we surrender to disparity and depression, we are spiritually dying and adding no value to our relationship. These are the kind of people who are consumed by their attitude to be angry and bitter. In order to have a healthy relationship, there must be an attitude change.

Unhappy people are critical of their mate; they see a need to change them instead of themselves. They always seem to want something different, while those who are content know that they must deal with the world as it is and not necessarily as they would like it to be. They understand that life brings some joy, some frustration, some sadness, and some disappointment and some painful situations. But they are confident they can handle everything life deals them because of an inner sense of confidence and peace. I tend to think that the essence of peace, joy and contentment is the unconditional love we have for our mate in our lives and their unconditional love they have for us.

Now on the other hand, people who expect to be happy everyday of their life are not really facing "life" reality. When you are learning to deal with the pain of the loss of happiness, knowing it will come around again is the most important thing. The lessons we learn now will lead us to our next level of happiness. You must be optimistic enough to know it is normal and human not to be happy every second of your life. When things in your relationship are not going as well as you want them to, you don't allow your frustration and disappointment to pull you apart. You adjust! I found out that painful situations do exist even in relationships and they are real and I also learned to deal with it, so you adjust! Happiness will return.

Any relationship, especially in marriage must grow. Rather than being an unhealthy and destructive dependency, a positive relationship must be a liberating experience that allows the partners not only to share their lives, but to realize their individual potential as well. There are adjustments in relationships, starting with our attitude, because when you're in love you want to live in harmony. If you enjoy exercise, you adjust yourself to that. If you enjoy movies, you adjust to taking two hours off to see that movie. If you want to keep thin, you adjust to not eating many sweets. As the two of you come together in one union you adjust relationship in marriage; the whole basis of life and happiness is to adjust.

If a relationship is built on "what am I getting?" all is lost from the start, the wrong attitude. A positive, happy relationship is built on love, trust, respect, and sharing. All relationships, from friendship to marriage, get deeper and better or they become shallow and fade. The ideal relationship should be a sharing of experiences, strengths, and hopes. It should be the sharing of our goodness with someone who appreciates our goodness and shares his or her goodness with us. I tend to appreciate that the essence of a good and happy relationship is the communication of feelings.

If we could only start communicating with each other, there would be less continues communicating of women with other women about our love issues, and as well there will be less continues communicating of men with other men about the same. What we must understand here is if we don't really start communicating with our own mate concerning our love issues, the greater the damage we are allowing to the relationship by those who are outside of the relationship. Less communicating in a positive way with our mate allows them to pass on a great deal of misinformation among others. Therefore we are allowing information that is not true or unhealthy for our relationship to be reinforced.

WHY SHOULD YOU LOOK BACK INTO YOUR PAST?

Understanding how certain aspects of the past have left their mark does not necessarily change the quality of one's life. Explanations such as, "I never developed self-confidence because my father was always criticizing me," or "I was afraid to speak my own mind because my mother was so domineering," can be reassuring insofar as they offer a rationale and justification for self-defeating attitudes and behaviors or for anger and resentments. But insight alone does not help.

Now it is certainly true that since the past is memory and the future is hope, this moment in time is the only one we ever really have. It is also true that the past is often used to avoid looking at the present, to protect one from an awareness of immediate pain or conflict, or from the anxieties inherent in change. Blaming our mate is also more comfortable than forcing answers to "what is there about my character, my psychological make-up, the way in which I relate, the assumptions I make about my self and others, the expectations I hold, the meaning I assign to what I experience, the self-deceptions I practice-which contribute to the continuation of my unhappiness and attitude behavior?

The memories of hurt and pain sometimes give rise to anger. This could be from some painful childhood feelings and/or incidents. Painful memories that are being kept inside can lead to suppressed love. Going through life blaming others always leads to anger, which can get out of control and very often lead you to act out inappropriately.

Suppressed resentments can make one's life miserable and often your mate and others around you. Not recognizing the hidden resentment that you are harboring restricts you from expressing yourself in a more positive way. Yet the impact of the past on our basic personality structure is such that we cannot dismiss it. I have come to understand that our present ways of experiencing and defining ourselves in various relationships and circumstances are an outgrowth of our earliest experiences in the world. Therefore for the most part what we experience today takes its meaning from the total context of our lives, not just the "here and now." Our reactions to events in our lives are based not only on the objective facts but also on the meaning we give to what we experience.

As we come to the understanding of how we got to be the way we are will not automatically make things better. It can provide foundation and direction for change in attitude and behavior, but if we are to truly grow in our relationship and change, the course of action we must take is to commit ourselves to the process with all its inherent fears. We must struggle against our own pride, our own selfishness, our drive for vengeance, and our wish to retreat to the safety of mother's arms.

Eliminate the blame and criticism that so permeated the relationship. In a word: STOP. So much criticism of our mate is in fact a cryptic expression of our needs. Criticism is the adult version of crying, nature's built-in distress signal for getting our mate's attention. In adulthood we translate our screeching, pathetic, incessant cries into language, inflicting our mates with pain in a warped effort to get them to meet our needs in a selfish way. This attitude embedded in all criticism is a wish or desire, just as a need not met stimulated the childhood crying. In an unbalance relationship, we expect our mate to meet our needs, as our parents did in childhood, and we fault them when they fail to meet them. In a balance relationship, our mates identify the needs hidden in our criticism and express them as desires followed by a request that they be met.

THE WRONG ATTITUDE IS WHAT CAUSES CONFLICT IN RELATIONSHIP

"If you don't like my attitude too bad, I am not going to change."

"Get off my back! I can't stand you."

"You will never change, you will always be foolish."

"You are so foolish, you can't do anything right."

"I hate you! My ex was a much better person."

"I need someone who can provide for me better than what you are doing."

"Why can't you be more like . . ."

"My family told me not to marry you."

OUR WORDS CAN HEAL OR
THEY CAN BE DESTRUCTIVE

Unhappy people with a bad attitude who are in a relationship should realize the danger of their tongue; a few words spoken in anger can destroy a relationship that may have taken years to build. So before you speak, you must realize that words are like fire and you can neither control nor reverse the damage they can do in a relationship. Damaging words can spread quickly and you cannot stop the consequences once they are spoken. To seek forgiveness later for the pain you have caused will not remove the destruction that has been done. We sometimes speak words in hurt and anger in hopes of making ourselves feel better, not realizing we are making a bigger mess of the situation. Know that words used in the wrong way can pull a person down; they can destroy and yes, even cause a death. Think before you speak. Ask yourself: is this what I truly want to say? Is it necessary? Is it kind?

People who speak careless words in conflict to hurt their mate thinking that they can apologize and seek their forgiveness later, don't realize the damage is done. Although they may forgive you, the scars you have caused remain. The Bible tells us in James 3:6. And the tongue is a fire, a world of iniquity: so is the tongue among our members, that it defileth the whole body, and setteth on fire the course of nature; and it is set on fire of hell. (kjv.) Therefore the tongue is a little member of the body but can do damaging and destructive results to a couple's relationship.

Anyone who chooses to go into a relationship with drama, and in denial that there are problems from within, is denying themselves of peaceful surroundings. To choose to be in denial of a drama filled life causes your mate to be uncomfortable with the relationship. People with bad attitudes are often making excuses for their action by saying, "I just can't help it; this is who I am." Or "I don't mean anything by it; sometimes I just use a poor choice of words."

They are in denial of their problem as well as being destructive to their relationship. They damage the relationship further by saying "there is nothing wrong with me, it must be you." They often place the blame on others. People, who have so much drama in their lives cause conflict with their mate, are hurting inside and their hurt will cause others to hurt. "People, who are hurting, hurt other people.

CONFLICTS ARE REAL
EVEN IN LOVING RELATIONSHIPS

There will be conflicts in a loving relationship. Every relationship has its share of conflict and the solution is not the avoidance nor elimination of conflict, but the constructive and productive management of differences. Adjustments are necessary in any relationship, and it starts with our attitude.

Conflict in any relationship is real. It happens when two people set out to share a life together in a significant way. When two persons try to relate "from the center of their beings," allowing each other to be their own person expressing that uniqueness, they are bound to have differences. If we care about ourselves, we care about our feelings and about something that means a great deal to us, these differences are going to cause disagreement within the shared life. The same time we care about another person, with whom there is a disagreement with about a value, a clear difference of opinion. There could be a distinctly different set of experiences being shared. Thereby we have a dual collision or conflict: one within the self, and one with the person whom we care about. To make things more complicated, there are feelings about each level of conflict, and those feelings leave us confused and defensive, as well as angry, withdrawn or hostile toward our mate.

There are a host of emotions that come to the surface when we find ourselves in this situation, and we may have very little preparation in our understanding to help us deal with the struggle that is created when these differences develop within the relationship. These differences of opinion or values many times will lead to disharmony and distance between the couple, and at that moment they may find themselves unable to come to a constructive approach that will lead them back to intimacy.

We all are growing, and changing everyday. In our own significant ways, none of us is the same person today that we were yesterday. Because we are growing and changing, it is inevitable that we shall not always be in tune at every moment with those around us, and especially those we love. Sometimes there will be differentiated unity even in a loving relationship. As we are growing and changing in life, there must be an attitude adjustment for blending together in harmony.

The simple fact that we care about one another and are open to what is going on with the other person makes us more sensitive to change, difference, and the distance that develops with change. It is tempting to overlook the reality that the wonderful, exciting experience of harmony between couples is possible only because of the contrasts that exists between them. Harmony, after all, is not undifferentiated unity. It is made up of contrasts, which have somehow been brought together through skillful attention to the possibilities for blending together; those possibilities are dependent on the strength of contrast.

Allow me to present my analogy from a musical point of view. When you listen to some of your favorite music, whether it is of two or more voices or instruments, you are aware that it is the clarity and strength of their differences that contribute to the beauty of harmony. Without care, attention, and practice, their individual sounds will not come together in a way that is pleasant for anyone to hear. The wonder of a symphony requires a strong collection of differences, each free to express itself in its own way, coming together only at the risk of considerable disharmony and a series of efforts marked by frustration and discouragement.

A prolonged battle in loving relationships is the experience of very real differences between the couple that cares about each other. A disagreement, or argument, or explosion of anger may be about something that is only a symptom of the real conflict. These differences involve feelings, values, personal desires and perceptions. They can go as deep as a sense of identity, unspoken expectations in the relationship, and the inevitable process of change that happens in each of us, as well as between us. The experience of collision between the couple is an indication of distance in the relationship. The challenge in any relationship should be the will and desire to reduce the distance and increase intimacy that should be sought by the two, in other words, an attitude adjustment.

The human situation involves the two people in trying to overcome a sense of isolation from self and from each other. As they make that effort, out of great need and desire for unity with each other, they learn that the one to whom they are attracted to, see some things differently or disagree with them in important ways, which has caused a conflict in the relationship. In each clash there is heat and possible misunderstanding that has resulted in distance between the couple. In our moments of thoughtfulness and caring, we want to reduce that distance, and move toward the intimacy that pulled us together in the first place.

For your consideration in a heated disagreement, here are some suggestions of a more constructive approach to reduce distance between the couples that care about each other, which may be used:

Darling you know, we are both "right" about some things.
My love, we are both "wrong" about some things.
Darling we both must understand that we see some things differently, because we are different persons with different backgrounds and perspectives.
My love, both of us want to achieve something for ourselves, and I understand that.
Darling each of us has much to contribute to a shared solution to our problem in a constructive manner.
My love, I believe we both want to get pass this problem that separates us and move toward intimacy.

One of the basic emotions in a prolonged battle, of course, is anger. Most of us are not very good at knowing what to do with our anger. In trying to fix a mess from our own understanding, we make a bigger mess. I have often used this three-step system (I learned from a fellow Minster and friend) in my ministry during many of my counseling sessions with couples.

The first step in dealing with anger is: Try to acknowledge your anger to each other as soon as you become aware of it. This approach allows it no time to build up; built up anger becomes suppressed anger, which can be explosive anger and this could be damaging to the relationship. A precondition to this step is the acceptance of each other's right to get angry.

The second step in dealing with anger is: Renounce the right to vent your anger on each other. To tell the other that you are angry is not the same as venting. Since acting out angrily would be damaging to the one you love, you should say to the other, "I am getting angry with you, but you know that I am not going to attack you." This approach is to keep your mate from going on the defensive, which could lead to retaliatory anger and more likely a fight.

The third step in dealing with anger is: Ask your mate to help you to deal with the anger that has developed. Now you may think that this approach may seem strange, if you are angry with your mate, and you appeal for their help in fixing the problem, it is very much in their interest to respond in a positive manner. Most of the time it is necessary to get negative feelings off of your chest, but not to use your mate for that purpose, but in a constructive manner. Your mate is not to be used as a "garbage dump" for your personal "emotion refuge."

The agreement that is basic on my suggestive three-step system includes a commitment to continue working on each of your anger situations that develop between you until the both of you are able to clean up the situation that is a hinder in your relationship. By working together on your anger, you will have the opportunity to learn more and more about possible anger-producing actions that can and will occur between you in any relationship. This can result in gaining the power, based on the right knowledge, in how to avoid major crises in your relationship. The key point to this system is that each person involved does not suppress their feelings, but accept them and resolve them together. This action, if done in a loving and caring way is what moves them back toward increased intimacy. There is a statement that is so fitting in this chapter, by James Baldwin, "Love does not begin and end the way we seem to think it does. Love is a battle, love is war: love is growing up." Should you not want to be happy in your relationship? This can only happen when the two of you are communicating, working together in a loving and caring way for its existence.

If you change, your relationship changes. People often feel stuck when things are not going particularly well in their relationship because they think they can't make it better. Their spouse has a negative attitude, not willing to go to a marriage counselor, or even sit down and discuss the problems in the relationship to help make it better. So my question is, how can things get better if our attitude is negative and we are not willing to communicate? Things get better because you change, and as a result of your changing, your marriage will get better.

If you are willing to go through the pain that accompanies change, your marriage will improve and the pain will soon disappear. Now, on the other hand, if your attitude remains negative and you decide to reject the pain that comes with change, you will still have the pain of being in an unhappy and unfulfilling marriage. There are few things that are equal to the special joy that is realized in having a good and happy marriage.

CHAPTER 4
LET'S TALK SEX;
CAN WE REALLY HAVE THIS TALK?

Can we have a genuine heart-to-heart discussion about sex? Yes, sex! Although such a subject may be a total embarrassing topic to discuss, there may be some good understanding that can be realized from this discussion. As a pastor and spiritual guide, my question is, "Should we not be able to give a more sound and informative spiritual insight to such a discussion as this?" Of course our talk should be based most of all upon biblical principles, which is where we will find the foundation of our discussion. Should not we, who are pastors and spiritual leaders of the church, be able to give a more sound Biblical informative understanding to a subject such as this than one who may not have such a calling upon his or her life? In the church as there is outside of the church, are men and women young and old, teens and preteens who are struggling with sexual issues, as well as married and unmarried couples. Just maybe if we are more proactive in a foundational discussion with this subject matter as we are about other subject matters, our followers who seek the truth will be greater. In my discussion about this topic, my determination is to report to you my understanding on the facts as I can, in as nonjudgmental way as possible.

There is no issue in our culture that has been more misunderstood on all sides than sexual relations. From the puritanical views of our ancestors to today's promiscuous and negative attitudes, irresponsibility and abuse of sex, much damage has been done to relationships in the name of sex. Yet a healthy sexual relationship based in Christian views is a foundation of any good marriage.

Today, 72% of black babies are born to unmarried mothers, according to government statistics. Most of African American young ladies don't think that they have to be married, but they fail to understand that children need a mother and father. A mommy can't give it all, and nether can a daddy. Not by themselves. The real truth to be understood is that you can only give that which you have, and a mother cannot give all that which a man can give. A truly involved father figure offers more fullness to a child's life.

Statistics show and give us a clear understanding of just what fullness means. Children of unmarried mothers of any race are more likely to perform poorly in school, they are nine times more likely to drop out of school, they are twenty times more likely to end up in prison, they are more likely to use drugs, be poor as adults and have their own children out of wedlock.

What our African American unmarried couples should be striving for is that marriage should be the "norm" in the black community rather than the exception. One of the most disturbing facts among us is that part of our community has lost its way. We have too many African American fathers who have abandoned their responsibility in their child's life.

During my teen years, there were three basic reasons for not having sex before marriage: (1) getting a girl pregnant, (2) venereal disease (this was before AIDS became the leading cause of death among blacks in the United States), and (3) the biblical condemnation. Now of course, premarital sex does risk pregnancy and venereal disease, but the reasons for avoiding premarital sex go far beyond these considerations. With the help of a physician and a free clinic, a couple can avoid having a baby. Antibiotics can cure most venereal diseases (except AIDS). But the timeless message of Scripture remains clear. The Bible clearly condemns sex prior to marriage.

If there be any among you who have, or are committing the act of fornication by engaging in sex before marriage, the word of God tells us it is a sin. God, who is Holy, condemns those who engage in premarital sex as being unclean and unholy. Let's be real!! No matter how good it may feel to you by committing the act, or how well relieved one may be from engaging themselves in it, the facts remain the same, "sin." God gave us our sex drive not to make us miserable but it is to bring us fulfillment in marriage. As I stated in an earlier chapter, the sexual act is not for just making babies but is also intended for pleasure between a husband and wife.

In order to become what we are supposed to be morally and sexually, we have become what we are not and should be, irresponsible, immoral and sinful. We are sexual human beings, and our sexuality is a part of the pulsating energy of life, which we express through mind, body, and soul. Our yearning for sexual union is a core manifestation of our drive to achieve union with our partner only in marriage. True sex is "natural," and our goal should be to return to a purer perception and experience of it to its joys and pleasures. Sexuality is the spiritual center of partnership and the foundation on which trust and commitment rest.

The word of God reads like this in Matthew and the 19 Chapter; "And for this cause shall a man leave father and mother, and shall cleave to his wife: and they twain" (two) "shall be one flesh? Wherefore they are no more twain" (two,) "but one flesh. What therefore God hath joined together, let not man put asunder". Matt.19: 5-6. (kjv.) Therefore it is the will of God that a sexual union to be in marriage consisting of a husband and wife. It is for the couple to experience closeness, that they be united, to be "one fresh." Sex before marriage is fornication and sinful, being that as it is the word of God calls for us to abstain from fornication and repent. Please read. Acts: 15:20.1Cor.6: 18. And 2Cor.12: 21 and 2Cor. 13:1.

God created our sexuality. It is one of Gods gifts to His humans, and therefore it is good. When fit into the larger framework of human meaning and honor, it shaped to serve our noblest values and deepest needs, sex is responsible. Sex is uniquely designed for and carries the potential of fostering the deepest of interpersonal relationship in marriage. Therefore in a human and Christian sense, through good sex it helps us to achieve personal growth, true intimacy, committed love, marriage and family. However if sex is given a different meaning other than this, used selfishly, exploitatively, or without regard to consequences, sex is irresponsible and therefore harmful and sinful.

It has become common for people in general to engage in sexual intercourse in this twenty first century more than ever before. People are now more open about having sex than ever, even our young people are as sexually active if not more than their parents are. Sex is all over our TV sets, the Internet, even our cell phones. A six or seven year old child can get all of the information about sex as they desire with pictures, just by pulling it up on their cell phone. Children and young people as well as older adults are more anxious about indulging in the experimentation of sexual relationships with different people, than in times past. If the world stands, we are just beginning to comprehend the changes in relationships that have resulted from this sexual revolution. Believe it or not, we are living in a time of dramatic transition and sexual tension as never before.

THE DAMAGING AND DESTRUCTIVE FACTS OF . . . PREMARITAL SEX.

The consequences of such a culture as this, we now realize that sexually transmitted diseases are more common than ever before and, due to HIV/AIDS, more alarming than ever before. And in this day and time AIDS still remain the leading cause of death among African American women between the ages of 25 and 34. It's the second leading cause of death among black men between the ages of 35 to 44. Today, 47 percent of the HIV cases in the United States are African Americans, even though African Americans make up only 13 percent of the population. Yes, only 13 percent. Too many of our young women are giving birth to babies with mental and physical challenges and other birth defects due to the use of drugs and from sexually transmitted diseases. The one sure way to avoid AIDS and other sexually transmitted diseases and its complications is complete abstinence till marriage.

Any person who suspects that he or she might have HIV or any other venereal disease should contact a physician or a public health clinic immediately. Please do not prolong the wait. The longer you wait, the worse a sexually transmitted disease gets and the greater the chances of you spreading and infecting others. An infected mother can transmit these diseases to her unborn child. The infectious agents pass from the mother's bloodstream into the bloodstream of the fetus. The child may be infected any time from six weeks to the time of delivery. If the mother's infection is not treated in the first six weeks, the probability of stillbirth more than quadruples. These diseases do not cure themselves, although with some of these diseases the symptoms may disappear. The care and treatment that your local health department provides is absolutely free, and the records they keep are not made known to the public.

Young people, as well as the older adults today, for the most part remain unmoved by pious parching. Honest answers based on proven facts, however, will impress contemporary young people. In today's times no longer do young people ask, "Is it right or wrong?" but "Is it right for us in our relationship? Will it strengthen or weaken our relationship?" And with so many of them there is no question of any kind, they just say, "let's just do it anyway, because it feels right." A few years ago I was reading in the newspaper about a survey that was conducted on premarital sex. The finding from this survey was very moving. The report from this study on teen-age sexuality states that there is more sex, more pregnancies, more abortions, and fewer marriages today than ever before in history. More and more of today's young people question traditional morality. This approach makes a psychological question out of what otherwise would be a moral one.

It is not just a matter of whether or not people engage in premarital sex, but the disadvantage can be how often and with how many partners it occurs. If young people have sex with only one person before marriage, the disadvantages listed will apply, but the toll will not be as great as when there have been multiple partners.

People today are more sexually active than ever, young and the older adults as well. Studies that are being done today shows that preteen sex is on the rise. Children as young as nine years old (mainly little girls) are engaging in sex at an alarming rate.

There are studies that show premarital sex increases the risk of cervical cancer among young women who engage in sex with multiple partners. About the time menstruation begins, the entire endocrine system is being stabilized and the finishing touches are being put upon the development of the uterus, fallopian tubes, and ovaries. It is said that the cervix is extremely vulnerable during this time. If it is exposed to semen, whether from one or multiple partners, it can set the stage for what is called, carcinoma (cancer) of the cervix later on in life.

Semen contains so-called "antigens" that sensitize the cervix and may cause abnormal development when a young girl is exposed to it too early, too often, and by multiple sexual partners. Research shows that the younger a girl becomes sexually active and the more partners she has and the more frequent a girl's exposure is during those years, the higher her chances are of contracting cervical cancer during ages 40 to 45.

THESE ARE MORE DISTURBING FACTS CONCERNING HIV

By race/ethnicity, African Americans face the most severe burden of HIV in the United States (US). At the end of 2007, blacks accounted for almost half (46%) of people living with diagnosis of HIV infection in the 37 states and 5 US depended areas with long-term, congenial, name-based reporting. In 2006, blacks accounted for nearly half (45%) of new infections in the 50 states and the District of Columbia. Even though new HIV infections overall have been roughly stable since the early 1990s, compared with members of the races and ethnicities they continue to account for a higher proportion of cases at all stages of HIV-from new infections to deaths.

In 2006 studies show that black men accounted for two-thirds of new infections (65%) among all blacks. The rate of new HIV infections for black men was 6 times higher than white men, nearly 3 times that of Hispanic/Latino men, and twice that of black women.

In 2006 studies show that black men who have sex with men according to the Center for Disease Control men having sex with men represented 63% of new infections among all black men, and 35% among all having sex with men. HIV infection rates are higher among black men having sex with men compared to other men having sex with men. More new HIV infections occurred among young black men having sex with men (ages 13-29) than among any other age racial group of men having sex with men.

In 2006 studies show that HIV infections for black women was nearly 15 times as high as that of white women and nearly 4 times that of Hispanic/Latino women.

Due to the destructive behavior and irresponsibility as well as accountability, African Americans continue to experience higher rates of sexually transmitted diseases (STDs) than any other race/ethnicity in the US. The presence of certain STDs can significantly increase the chance of contracting HIV infection. A person who has both HIV infection and certain STDs has a greater chance of infecting others with HIV.

I had only one more patient to visit that afternoon before going home for the evening. She had requested pastoral counseling so that she could have the opportunity to accept Christ into her life; this young child said that as far as she can remember she has only been to church three times in her life. She stated that her mother has been on drugs and has lived an irresponsible life long before she was born. She is one of two children; her brother is five years older.

As I entered her room she was so happy to see me and gave me a big hug and said "Pastor, I am so glad that you came to see me today, how are you doing?" I replied, "Well darling to see you with that big smile on your face, I am doing very well, you have truly made my day." This little girl is fifteen years old and five months pregnant with her second child.

She was admitted into the hospital as she often does for prenatal care of the unborn child that she is carrying and to receive treatments for the disease that she also has. This little child was diagnosed with HIV. But I am very pleased to report that the infectious agents from this disease did not pass from the mother's bloodstream to the fetus.

She shared with me the disgusting story of sexual abuse that she endured as far back as she could remember and her mother continues use of drugs. The mother's drug addiction caused a negative impact on their family life, and the mother's live-in boyfriend "Walter" only added to that negativity. Many times when the mother was unable to have sex with him, or when he had no sexually desires for the mother, she would allow Walter, the live-in boyfriend to go into her daughter's room and he would force himself on her. This started she said when she was only ten years old and has been on going since then. The only reason this little girl could give for the mother allowing this man to do these evil things to her daughter was, because she did not want to lose her man.

This man is the father of her first child. At first this little girl would cry out to her mother; " Mommy, mommy!! Make him stop he is hurting me." The mother being high on drugs as usual would only reply by saying, "It is OK baby, Walter loves you just like he loves me, he is not going to hurt you, it will be all right." But she would cry out even more. "Mommy please make him stop, I don't want him doing this to me. Please, make him stop!!" The mother would only insist that this little girl would allow this man Walter, the live in boyfriend to carry out his shameful act of sexual abuse on her daughter. The mother even had the audacity to tell her daughter; " Mommy loves you baby and Walter loves you too, he is not going to hurt you, don't make him feel bad." As this child was trying to tell her traumatic story of sexual abuse and neglect, I was able to observed the painful expression on her face and the difficultly she was experiencing, as she would attempt to speak of certain critical details of the abuse.

This child said that she would worry about this man all the time. "I never felt safe in my own home, I stayed outside as long as I could, it was like I was being hunted all the time, I felt like an animal. There were times I would be in the bathroom trying to take a bath for school and he would come in there and mess with me. He would force himself on me, and do this to me on the floor in the bathroom before I went to school. But then I finally gave up. I got to where I would let him do whatever he wanted to. Trying to keep this secret of abuse and pain inside of me was pulling me apart. All of this had me feeling so bad about myself, so many times I thought about committing suicide everyday."

These statements were uttered by a little girl, (let's just call her Mary,) who never before had been willing to talk to anyone as she did with me about her shameful experience of child neglect and sexual abuse. I had counseled her on the importance of releasing those negative feelings, to free herself of the pain of trying to hold all the hurt and abuse inside of her. I assured her by trying to keep the abuse and shame a secret is a false sense of responsibility. So many people try to live with the secret and shame of their abuse not realizing the shame will poison your thoughts and actions. When you voice the ugliness of it, it frees you. The devil wants you to keep the traumatically stressful hurt and shame within a secret, because it torments and it breeds negative thoughts and wrongful actions.

Mary told me of the disturbing and dramatic shameful story of incest that she also endured, it became all too common to her. This was sexual abuse on this child by her brother and one of the uncles in the family. This little girl was being victimized in her own home, a place where she should have been safe and free to be a child. She never felt safe; children should feel safe and protected in their own home. The major consequence of being violated as this is terror. The person who has felt helpless and victimized is traumatically and chronically stressed. They feel isolated, withdrawn from reality and lonely. Sexual abuse violates the core of one's being, their physical, emotional and spiritual boundaries. The betrayal makes it even more shocking. This child's life has been a disparaging nightmare.

There were others as well as myself who have on a number of occasions tried to get the mother admitted to a center for counseling and drug treatment but of the two times she checked herself in, she would not follow through with the program. Although I have put in much time in trying to work with this family, I have been unsuccessful but my main focus was to do all I could to help little Mary and her children to make sure they were safe and out of harms way. After many difficulties and hindrances, in trying to work with a family that was habitual drug users and abusers, there was not very much progress on their part. But I was finally able to get Mary and her little babies out of that abusive environment and place them in a nice home with a well adjusted loving family. These are people I know very well, they are an older couple in their mid to late 60's who are very active in the church and love the Lord.

Little Mary is a young lady now and she is very happy, she and her two children are doing just fine and yes, she gave birth to a healthy baby girl. She now has two very beautiful little girls, and we are so happy to report that Mary is free of HIV, she is working in the church with her new mom and dad, and she loves life. Here is what she said to me the last time I talked with her; " I have been choosing between varying courses of actions in life since I am now on a new start in life. And my new parents who have confidence in me, and my judgment. My new church friends and church have the same high standards that my parents have for me."

"There is no special virtue in my chastity. It is what I have chosen as the way I want for my life. Pastor Johnson, I now believe in fidelity and my loyalty to God, to my parents, to my sense of what is right, and to my future husband and our marriage. What others call "fun" and "messing around" I find it not to be enjoyable, for I prefer keeping my life clean, open and holy. You see, the Lord is rebuilding my life anew and for this I am grateful. I remember one of the many things you told me pastor Johnson, when I first came to you for help, you said that I should not allow my mistakes and faults to dictate my future. This journey which I have chosen for my life is of my choosing and I know that I can do all things through Christ which strengthens me."

I was informed a few years ago since the time of this shameful abuse, that Mr. Walter, the live in boyfriend and abuser, died in prison after being abused himself often physically and sexually by the inmates at the institution where he was placed to serve his time for the crime he committed. It is not known how he died. We understand that the mother of little Mary has also passed which was due from the neglect of her health and drug abuse. We have no known where about of the brother and uncle of little Mary; it is our hope that if they are still living that they are receiving some critical counseling and treatment for their problem.

Sexual abuse is the most shameful kind of abuse, especially when it is committed on the young and those who are unable to defend themselves. It has the greatest element of betrayal in it. The person abusing you says loudly and clearly, you are only an object to be used for my need. You are not valuable as a person in your own right. And the person who has been sexually abused is also bound to their offender in a very powerful way.

Sexual and physical violence are devastating forms of abandonment. The child is left alone. The child is a victim of the offender's shameless needs. They are used and abused. Sexual and physical violence is about the silence of nights spent holding in screams, holding back their tears; holding in one's own victimized self.

TO KEEP FROM GOING TOO FAR, IS UP TO YOU.

To avoid going too far in a relationship, there must be a mindset based on Biblical teaching concerning premarital sex. You should develop a positive feeling of self-worth, ideals and values. It is one of the most important factors in avoiding premarital sex. And also open communication with your partner regarding your standards and Christian values is an excellent way to prevent arousing situations from happening. If you live up to your own values and standards, others will think highly of you, but even if they do not; an inner conflicts will not tear you up inside. You will respond to others opinion of yourself with personal integrity and self-confidence. Your appearance, abilities, or social acceptance will not worry you, leaving you free to love as you choose, to work, and to play free of guilt.

Sadly too many of our young girls are attracted to thugs, bad boys who run the streets, steal, sell drugs, and are "banging". These young girls become hard, cold and indifferent toward life and the innocence of the child and young lady that she really should be about. This kind of attitude leaves them in a more violable position. Single mothers are surging in the US. Some studies show now that it is about 71% for Blacks, 28% for Whites and 50% Mexicans. These young females are giving birth out of marriage at an alarming rate. One of the key points I try to make clear in my book for all of our young girls and ladies is this; that you should develop a positive feeling of self-worth, as well as having high standards and values. I want you to love yourself, to protect yourself not only from having babies outside of marriage, but also from sexual viruses. And it goes further than a condom. We want married women to know that a wedding ring or the certificate doesn't protect you from HIV. Ignorance does not protect you from this virus; it will only make you more susceptible.

To our dear sisters; you are not and should not see yourself just as an object to be used for someone's needs to release themselves in. Holding to the high standards and values that you have for yourself is one of the most important factors in avoiding premarital sex. And keeping in mind that you are a valuable and worthy person in your own right. And you do not need to place yourself in situations where you cannot be affirmed or where you feel uncomfortable.

Therefore having said that, it is always wise for you to set up rules for the proper conduct in advance for yourself and your mate. Think through your own standards, and develop criteria for your actions based on your personal values and the word of God. These should be standards that you would be proud to discuss with anyone. Develop a specific plan to follow so that you can continue in a healthy growing relationship with a member of the opposite sex without compromising yourself. After you have carefully thought out your standards, plan how you might maintain them. Think of the difference this could make in good healthy relationships.

You should choose carefully the person that you intend to be in a relationship with. Carefully and prayerfully select someone hopefully who has Godly standards that they live by on a daily basis. It is a good idea to choose someone who also has some of the same interests and ideals as well as values that you do. Be sure to avoid situations that may be designed to stimulate sexual pleasure. And learn to control your own sexual desires. You do not have to give in to your sexual urges just because you have them. It doesn't matter whether you are married or single. From time to time you will have to control your sexual desires. Even married couples have to do so. The wife may be sick and in a hospital for two or three weeks or the husband may have to take an extended trip out of town; self-control must be exercised during such time.

Remember, sex is a gift from God. He did not give you your sexual drive to make you miserable, it is pleasurable and to be enjoyed the way God intended it to be, that is in the appropriate time after you have taken your mate in marriage. God created the sexual desire in you, He can and will control the desire in you if you are willing to allow Him to.

"Delight yourself also in the Lord; and He shall give thee the desires of thine heart. (Psalms 37:4). If you love what God loves, He will give you His desire that He loves and wants you to have.

Ask God for guidance. Ask Him to help you find His will for your life. If you and your partner discuss and pray about your future together, it will produce a bond of conscience between you that can serve as a barrier against temptation. Discuss your relationship in terms of the three of you, "God, you, and I."

CHAPTER 5

THE NEED TO BE:
LOVED, NURTURED, COMFORTED
AND APPRECIATED.

What is missing the most in your relationship that deprives you from being happy fulfilled and satisfied? Not so long ago I was teaching a men's class in one of my out-reach ministries that I founded, in the city of Mobile, Al. One evening during our class session I decided to ask the above question to the class, the responses were overwhelming. The response and participation from those men that evening was more than I had expected, I felt they were truthful in their concerns and realized, "these men were hurting."

A middle aged man in the group stood up and said; "Elder Johnson, I am glad you asked that question and I would like to give my answer to it. The thing that makes me so dissatisfied with the attitude of my wife is that she doesn't seem to understand. I am a man who works hard every day to take care of my family, and if it is not enough I will do more. But when I come home from work she makes me feel so unappreciated. I am one who loves my wife very much and try to meet her needs. I feel my primary goal is to make her happy to the best of my ability. We have five children and four grandchildren, our two youngest children and one grandchild are still at home with us."

"The thing that made me happy the most was at the end of each day of enduring the competitiveness in the mean world of work, was when I get home my efforts and struggles were justified by my wife's appreciation. Elder Johnson, in a very real sense my wife's love and appreciation fulfilled me and it was the reward that made my labor worthwhile. But now when I come home from work it is like I am unappreciated, and sometimes she makes me feel defeated by saying "You here already?" And my last point is this; I feel if a man who is hard working and supporting his family is unappreciated by his wife he feels that his work is meaningless. He comes to the understanding that the unhappiness of his wife somehow confirms his defeat. If she is unhappy, to me it is a sign that she is saying that I am a failure, so why should I bother to keep trying to do more? I am unappreciated for what I am doing already."

A young man in the back of the room (whom I learned later that evening was a high school teacher) stood up and said; "I feel that as a black man and I think I speak for most of us, and I am talking about we brothers who are taking responsibility and going to work every day and paying the bills, providing for his family and doing all those things any man of integrity will do. As a whole we are not appreciated for our efforts and sacrifices as white men are by their wives. Most black men are overworked, overstressed and underpaid, and when we come home we are unsupported and unappreciated by our women. Instead of being rewarded with emotional support and love, we are getting blamed by our wives for not being able to provide them those materialistic things that our white brothers are doing for their wives. Pastor, so many of our women are shallow, there is no genuine sincerity in them."

"Relationships in our community are becoming increasingly difficult because mates expect too much of us. Yes we would like to be the sole provider in our households, it give us a strong sense of being but on a more deeper emotional level, as the brother said earlier we feel defeated when we see the unhappiness and unfulfillment in our mates. We could appreciate the fact that if our mates were able to stay at home and be full time wives and mothers instead of working on a job all day, afterward coming home and fulfill the needs of a stay at home wife and mother. But in today's economy it is somewhat difficult. In today's economy more than ever it takes a two-career marriage to keep your head above water. I can understand some of the frustration of my wife; I also understand that we are who are in our own relationship, a couple who is committed in trying to make the best of what we have. So I feel that we need to appreciate each other more in our relationships for our efforts and sacrifices, then our marriages would be happier."

In so many of the classes I teach, even in some of my speaking engagements, I record the sessions for my personal use. I find the information that comes out of these meetings to be tremendously helpful. This gives me good feedback and the understanding into my search to be even more helpful in my dialogue with others. I believe if men and women are to be happy and to succeed in supporting each other in their relationship, it is essential that they take the necessary steps in relationship skills, for renewed romance and intimacy. In each case when they take advantage of these skills, we realize great improvement in the relationship.

As these men were venting out their frustration I could sense, they seemed to be saying that as black men we are all out of work. We no longer have the job we once held as the breadwinner, husband and father. We are not appreciated as provider and protector. Although these men are still doing what they have been doing, going to work providing for their households, giving them the love and support they need that helps make a good family environment. But in today's time of competitiveness and materialism, it is not enough to make their mates happy. The downside to personal unhappiness, unfulfillment and unappreciative, is the dramatic change in the relationship that results in unfaithfulness from both sides with so many of our couples.

There was one man in the class who stood up and said; "Elder Johnson, I can agree on what these brothers are saying and I am glad to be a part of this class and give my input into this discussion. I believe that most men don't leave their wives because they no longer love them; I believe most of these men leave because they are no longer able to meet their mate's needs or satisfy them. I also agree with these brethren, in that we are not trying to make any excuse not to do our best. As men it gives us great satisfaction in doing our very best to provide for our family. But it seems like to some of our sisters, marriage is not that important to them anymore."

"The fact that so many of our sister's shallowness comes from what they see on TV and from what they read in these magazines; they are not able to collect the positive things from what they see or read what can be good and reasonable for their relationship, instead they want it all. Therefore this is what causes them not to be genuine and sincere in their complaint. Our mates must understand most of us will never be able to look like or be like what they see on TV, the internet or read in magazines. Neither will we ever be able to provide or give them all of what they see on TV, pull up on the internet or read in the magazines. But we will do, and are doing our best to provide for them, and maybe with a little appreciation for our efforts, it can be the push we need to go farther and do more."

Generally speaking, it could be stated that men give up on their relationship when they feel powerless, or that there is nothing more they are able to do to succeed in being appreciated. When the man feels that he is continually being disappointed and hurt in relationships, he will also resent feeling obligated to satisfy his mate's needs. Both persons in the relationship have somewhat the same needs when it comes to being loved, nurtured, appreciated, and respected. These are needs that both persons should continue to look for in the relationship, not to be put aside. No one should expect to be happily in love and married, if you are putting aside the very essence of those things that give your marriage its true meaning of intimacy.

In the early stages of a marriage the coming together in union is incredible and energizing to both man and woman. Before a woman knows a man, she expects or hopes that he will be the one to fulfill her needs. When she responds with appreciation, it encourages him to think "She is appreciating me so much for the little things I am doing, wait until she realizes the big things I am going to do; she will really be happy."

Men and women both shift in a variety of ways; they change over the course of their relationship. In most cases, they are completely unaware of how they are contributing to the problem of the relationship. They honestly believe that it is only their mates who are different. In many cases when our mate changes, it is easy to misinterpret their motives and feel that he/she does not love us as much as before.

Although these changes are largely unconscious, a man who doesn't understand them may become resentful and hold back. Be encouraged, all is not lost, and with the right understanding through dialogue, and greater insight into the relationship, you can immediately begin to bring back the woman you fell in love with. As you are learning to give your love in a specific way, a man can help his mate cope with and overcome these changes. Without this understanding, you will tend to react instinctively and in most cases, you will only make things worse. Even though your intention is to help your mate love you better; she eventually begins to pull away.

When a woman changes, it doesn't mean that she is not in love with her husband. Even still, in his quiet moments, a man wonders where the woman he chose to marry has gone. Here are some thoughts and feelings men have about the ways in which their wives change. These are some of the common comments and complaints you will most likely hear:

"In the beginning, my wife was always in the mood to have sex. She loved it. But now when I ask her it seems like she is never in the mood. I get tired of begging, I just don't bother anymore."

"Before we got married, my wife was always happy and so excited to see me. But now when I come home from work, she is always complaining about something or she is cool and distant. I have more problems on my job than I need, I don't want to come home and hear her complaining to me about what I am not doing right. "

"When my wife and I first married she was always happy, but now she tries to make me feel like I am the problem, it seems like all my wife does is complain about how I am not doing enough around the house. If I try to do anything, it seems that it's not good enough or she will try to make a big deal out of anything that I do, nothing is ever good enough."

"My wife used to really appreciate all of the places I would take her. But now, no matter where I take her it is not good enough, "Why did you have to come to this place." She wanted to go to someplace else. I just don't want to be bothered anymore in trying to please her."

"Before my wife and I got married, no matter what I did she was happy, she was easy to please and she was always appreciative of whatever I would do for her but now, when I open the car door for her it's like I'm expected to do that but it doesn't really matter."

"In the beginning of marriage, my wife loved me unconditionally. I felt good because around her I could just be myself. Now she is always trying to change me, and complaining about why I am not like this guy, or that guy or even her ex. Sometime I just don't want to be around her so I don't have to hear her mouth."

"My wife used to be so happy with whatever I did. It seemed like I could do no wrong as far as she was concerned. No matter what I did, it was good enough; I looked forward in coming home from work to my wife. But as soon as I get home now, she acts like she is not happy to see me, she starts complaining about little things and trying to make a big deal out of it. Sometimes I feel like I have to hide from her, I just don't want to come home to another boss. She doesn't realize that I have to go on fishing trips just to get away from her."

"When my wife and I first married, she was so happy to have me in her life. I really felt I made a difference. Now it seems our marriage is not that important anymore, she is never satisfied."

The common theme you have in each of these examples is that the man feels his wife wants more in the relationship, and she appreciates less. As we have seen from the beginning, he felt appreciated and loved, but over time, his feeling was lessened. Although from his point of view, her behavior may not have changed much in some ways, but the sisters' attitude has and she is much less supportive of him and his concerns.

In the early days of the relationship, the woman was very appreciative of whatever the man did. Over time as the relationship progressed and they married and moved in together, the "now" wife, grew less of her husband's emotional needs and view other things in the marriage more important as a way of expressing her love. However, chances are she is probably not aware of her husband's desires, so when he points it out to her, she misunderstands and resists. Without understanding how men are different, it is hard for her to validate his driving need for appreciation. But when the woman doesn't understand a man's deeper need for acknowledgment, he inevitably feels taken for granted.

The same common "humanly" mistake is made many times over. Once the couple is married, sometimes the wife does not realize that her husband stills needs her appreciation and acknowledgment. She assumes her job now is to do others things to express her love. What she doesn't know is that her husband would rather she do less of those things and appreciate him more as the man in her life.

Through practice, the wife can learn to respect her husband's sensitivities, in a real sense to acknowledge him as the man in her life through love and appreciation, is his "sacred circles." As she learns to focus her efforts as a loving wife on supporting him in the way he needs it most love, appreciation and nurtured. She should practice appreciating what he is doing and restraining herself from criticism and too much advice. As she supports his sense of competence, she should immediately experience his increased involvement in the relationship.

When couples are not in the knowledge of how to be creative in working together to build lasting intimacy in their relationship, they inevitably begin to feel increasingly distant and estranged. Break-up so often is the only option they seem to have. Most couples never fully embrace the one who is their lifetime partner. Interestingly, they seem to reserve their embraces for sexual acts or for tragic moments in their lives or at funerals . . . . how tragic?

When they do not understand their differences in human need and desires then they are unable to fully support each other in the most meaningful ways. When a woman does not feel supported in the relationship, over time she will become unbalanced in the relationship. In an opposite way the same is true for the man, when he is not supported he becomes also unbalanced in the relationship.

Even though the two people may love each other very much, if the support factors of his and her needs are not being fulfilled, there is an emotional unbalance in the relationship. Disenchantment exists due to unmet needs. The inability of them failing to recognize and solve this problem is one of the biggest reasons why there are so many break-ups and divorces today.

While resentments are usually expressed in an emotionally unbalanced relationship, problems are always best modified when the couples learn to work together in creative coping strategies. When we are angry with our partners, we want them to stop doing something that annoys us.

If you yell loud enough, there is a possibility that you will get your way. Unfortunately, getting your own way reinforces your yelling even more. This is a short-term solution to your problem.

First of all most couples reciprocate the negative treatment they receive from one another. Yelling begets yelling. Name-calling begets name-calling. Withdrawal begets withdrawal. Punishment begets punishment. Loss of sexual interest can beget loss of sexual interest.

My second point is this: As they allow time to progress in their resentment; the efforts will intensify to punish one other. And their positive ways of relating with each other that once occurred now becomes blurred to them. Out of spite, they give less and less in the relationship, they talk less, play less, touch less and they accompany each other less. They should ask themselves, can there be any doubt that this degenerative process produces ever-increasing anger, hurt, and resentment among us? Surely there must be a better way the two of them can work together to change things for the better. This unbalance between the couple will continue unless a more positive approach is taken.

1. Disenchantment exists due to unmet needs. Problems can only be solved when we begin to start doing more of each other's true needs and desires.
2. Unfortunately, most people cannot understand or know his/her mate's needs or desires. We instead get angry at our mate for not "knowing" How can they not know if you don't tell them?
3. To tell your mate in a demanding way to "stop doing this" or "you must do better than what you are doing." This can invite an angry defense from them and blocks whatever flows of caring that may

still exist. You should take steps in learning how to motivate your mate to get more of what you need, not more of what you don't need.

4. Two of the most common needs that are expressed from couples are, more honest communication and more intimacy. There is no true human need that cannot be met, by any person, if the will and commitment to meet that need exists. If the will to love exists, the know-how can be acquired.

Not too long ago a couple came to me for counseling; let us call them, Rob and Susan. After we had prayer, I said to Rob, "Brother Rob I am reading my notes from the day of your call, you stated that you feel Susan no longer wants to be married to you. This is very serious; please tell me what makes you think she does not want to be married to you?

"Pastor Johnson, Susan seems to be angry at me all the time, no matter what I do it is not good enough. She never wants to talk about whatever the problem is. There was the time after a hard day at work when I would come home to my wife, she would make me feel good and appreciated for my efforts. Now all she does is complains and try to start an argument with me about anything. Susan is always trying to make me feel like I am a failure and unappreciated, she doesn't seem to understand that although I am a man I have feelings also. Pastor Johnson, I go to work everyday and often I do overtime just to be able to provide for my wife, and try to make her happy by giving her the things she desire."

As he was speaking, I could see the hurt and pain in his eyes and at the same time see that this brother really loved his wife very much. As he continues; "Pastor Johnson, I don't ask much from my wife, and she knows this. She and I live a good life due to my hard work, I am able to take her on trips and vacations, places that she choose to go and we do so many wonderful things together. I come here today to try and save my marriage, but Susan's attitude is very damaging to our marriage. My faith in our marriage is somewhat shadowed in ways I cannot describe. In the past I would have done anything for my wife, but now I just don't understand my feelings for her, all because of her attitude." With his eyes full of water I said, "brother Rob, I think I have the picture now let me hear from your wife whom I believe loves you very much, and I know that the reason you are here today is because you still love your wife. I am sure that this is just some misunderstanding, and with you and your wife's help this can be worked out". I turn to Susan and ask her, "Sister Susan, can you share some light on this concern for me and please tell me how did we get to where we are right now?"

She said; "Rob is a good man,", patting him fondly on his thigh. "And I try to understand how hard it is for him and all he does. I did not know he doesn't think I don't appreciate him, he would tell me that I am so wrapped up in myself but I did not know I was making him feel that he is a failure and unappreciated. I wish that he could open up more, why can't he tell me he loves me? And I do know now I need to tell him that I love him also."

She continues; "Pastor Johnson, I know my attitude has not been pleasing to Rob and this could be the cause of the resentment he seems to have sometime, but if he could only open up to me more maybe my behavior would not have been as is was. I am sorry, and I now do understand how he feels, I love my husband very much." She turned to him and said; "Rob, I am truly sorry, will you please forgive me?"

Negativity, fallacies and finger pointing in a heated argument will not help a couple come to a peaceful solution of balance and intimacy. But this kind of negative approach of relating to your mate will increase the anger causing him/her to reciprocate the negative treatment they are receiving from you, which reinforces the same. Increased anger produces resentment, causing the both of you to build a wall of defense and withdrawal.

Therefore, before the couple can get back to intimacy, there must be a more positive approach taken by the both of them in a loving and caring way. The couple must work together to change the negative treatment, taking the necessary steps in learning to respect each other and appreciate the effort and value each brings into the relationship. Remember, you both want the same things, a loving, healthy relationship. You both need to be loved, nurtured, comforted and appreciated in a loving, healthy relationship. You ask what can I do? Learn to admit that you can, and might be, wrong.

After Rod and Susan made up with each other, I gave them some further techniques and skillful fundamentals that would aid them in maintaining a loving healthy relationship. In order for any couple to have a healthy relationship, you must work at it, and a good place to start is communication. Any time the two of you are willing to work things out, and you should, your relationship will get better. And if the two of you can't come to a peaceful solution go see a relationship counselor. Our goal here is to get back to intimacy. As I so often say, there are no perfect marriages/relationships, there will be challenges, in each life some rain must fall, and in all marriages/relationships you will have your share of problems. No relationships are without them, not any.

I knew a man who was the pastor at a local church that my church would fellowship with every three months, who was known for condemning others who had divorced or remarried, no matter what the reason was for their divorce. This pastor has always appeared to have a negative attitude for those in his congregation who was divorced or had remarried. No preacher was allowed to preach in his church that has had a divorce, even if the reason was your mate divorced you to be with another lover. I would often hear this man address his congregation in an "I am better that you attitude", "My wife and I have been married for more than thirty years, and we have never had a "cross word." Today that man and his ex-wife, yes! They are divorced.

And today, yes! This man has now remarried someone else, (the very thing he condemned others for doing) and his ex-wife has also remarried. Well, so much for not having a "cross word." I am not trying to make light of their situation; my point here is to get you to see that your relationship problems are similar to some other relationships. We understand to be in marriage, it has its own stages of development and its own issues. At times and for whatever reason, there may be an unbalance in your relationship, but for the most part if the two of you are willing, it can be fixed.

In the writing of my book I speak a lot on the subject such as, getting back to "intimacy", from a distant relationship, or from an unbalanced relationship to "intimacy" and so on. The one point that I want to make clear on this subject is when I speak of "intimacy," I am speaking of wholeness. In speaking on the word "intimacy" I am not talking about just sex, although sex is and should always be a very deep part of your relationship. In "intimacy" we are speaking of the whole, a communication in the essential innermost connection.

Intimacy is the most honest communication in love connecting. Intimacy is the connection in a relationship where the couple fully supports each other's emotional needs and desires, and having the understanding that your mates needs can change as we all are growing and changing in the relationship. In order for true "intimacy to exist, the both of you must have the right personality in a caring and loving healthy relationship. Each of you should enjoy the love of each other, which is what lovers do.

So put a smile on your face and show appreciation to your mate. Sometimes you should write a love letter to your mate, after all, this person is the love of your life. Do something nice for your spouse. The reason so many relationships break up, and many marriages fail, is that we take the other person for granted. One of the most important laws of human relations is "appreciate somebody and that person will become more to you; belittle somebody and that person become less to you." We take for granted the people who love us. In the midst of a most heated family argument, the both of you should stop and ask yourself these two questions: What can I do to make this relationship better?

What are the kind words and loving thing for me to do right now concerning my spouse? If we let that direct us, we would learn by coming out of ourselves. We must cure ourselves of selfishness or it will destroy us as a person.

I always make it a point, after preaching at most church service, to meet and general exchanges of greetings with the people. As I was standing near a young lady and greeting the people and enjoying their fellowship I could not help but overhear the sadness in this lady's voice. This lady was sitting looking down somewhat sadly at her purse and she said, plainly, "I know my husband can be more affectionate and tender to me. He's that way with our dog!" How much more wonderful and loving our relationships would be, if we humans could learn to embrace our mate's more lovingly and appreciate them.

CHAPTER 6

I MAY FORGIVE YOU, BUT!!
I WILL "NEVER FORGET" WHAT
YOU'VE DONE.

"For if ye forgive men their trespasses, your heavenly Father will also forgive you: But if ye forgive not men their trespasses, neither will your Father forgive your trespasses." Matt.6: 14-15. (kjv). Do-over; at one time or another we all wish we were given the opportunity for a do-over, and not have the mess-up held against us but a chance to "make it right." In the Holy Bible Jesus give us a startling warning about forgiveness: He tells us that if we refuse to forgive others, our heavenly Father will also refuse to forgive us. Why will He? Because when we don't forgive others, we are denying our common ground as sinners in need of God's forgiveness. God's forgiveness of sin is not the direct result of our forgiving others, but it is based on our realizing that forgiveness means it is easy to ask God for forgiveness of our sins, but difficult to grant it to others. Whenever we ask God to forgive us of our sins, we should ask ourselves, "Have I forgiven those who have wronged me?"

In my first book, *(AN ACCESSIBLE APPROACH TO OBTAIN WHOLENESS)* I tell the story of when I was a little boy down in Mississippi, how angry I was and found myself harboring some resentment and blame with some kids in our community who had stolen my bike. I was very angry and could not let it go. Although the kids had returned my bike unharmed and asked for forgiveness, at that time it was something I was too angry to do, they had stolen my bike!! A profound statement my mother said to me then was this: "Son, a big part of growing up is learning to forgive, even to those who took your bike."

Making peace with your partner is a personal challenge that will bring you enormous and lasting satisfaction. In order to clean up your relationship with your mate however, you must first make peace with yourself; it is the place where those internalized messages, feelings and conflicts are carried. Until you begin to work through that emotional backlog of accumulated resentments, a satisfying and harmonious relationship with your partner is almost a problem to accomplish.

The problem with stored or repressed hurt and pain is that it hinders you from real peace. Instead of permitting you to love and enjoy your mate, the hidden resentments will force you to find every opportunity to feel victimized by their actions, to blame them and to repeatedly act out the old negative patterns that you resent. How often have you said or felt one of the following about your partner?

1. "I try to be nice but my mate does things just to upset me."

2. "Sure I love my mate, but at the same time he/she drives me crazy."
3. "All my mate wants to talk about is the past, and he/she never stops reminding me about things that I would much rather forget."
4. "My mate is completely set in his/her ways. I just can't talk to him/her anymore."
5. "My mate just can't accept the fact that I am different from who he/she thought I was."

No matter how noble your intentions are to love and be loved by your mate, the resentments you harbor will sooner or later get in the way and hinder your noble intentions. So watch yourselves. "If your brother sins, rebuke him, and if he repents, forgive." Luke17: 3. (niv). To rebuke does not mean to point out every sin or wrong that a person does, but to remind them of their wrong deeds, with the purpose of restoring them back in fellowship with the Lord and fellow man. The word of God will have us to understand that when we feel a need to rebuke someone, we must check our own attitude; do we love the person? And are we willing to forgive?

LONELINESS IN THE RELATIONSHIP

People in relationships who are hurting and feel they are not getting the recognition and love they desire, can become lonely, bitter and unforgiving. This loneliness causes them to feel that the easiest choice for their loneliness is to just avoid the relationship within the relationship with their mate and live alone. The more he/she feels their needs and desires go unmet the more they will separate and retreat, not realizing this is pushing out the very love he or she needs so desperately.

When a person allows this kind of feeling to linger, they are always proving that they don't need their mate by saying words like; "I can do without you" This kind of attitude is only suppressing their true feelings of need. Un-forgiveness has a host of related negative emotional and physical feelings, one of them is loneliness, and loneliness causes you to reside in isolation and resentment in your relationship. You develop a false presentation of your feelings and desires. You tell your partner "I don't need you anyway." "Don't care what you thank." "I don't need anyone I can live all alone."

The lonely person feels guilty for needing love from their mate when they are not getting that recognition and love they desire, which result in him/her denying their needs. "I can live alone," they so proudly proclaim. Because they don't express their needs truthfully and let go the bitterness and hurt, they will continually be disappointed and hurt in the relationship. Their loneliness and bitterness can cause them to resent having a need to be loved by their mate; they feel that their needs are a sign of weakness.

This related emotional feeling of un-forgiveness causes inadequacy; they are unable to let go their resentment thereby, which allows them to express their needs and wants. "You disappointed me." You hurt me." "You belittled me." "I need you to respect me." "I need to be appreciated by you." "I need you to accept me." "I need to be loved, held and adored by you." "I need you to compliment me."

The loner must learn to share their needs with their mate and show their hurt and tears, not to be pitied, but to do a constructive management of the conflict. They should reveal their suppressed expectations and disappointments to their mate. To hold these feelings inside is what causes the grudges and resentment in the first place; remember grudge comes from an unforgiving heart. You must learn to forgive and let go these ill feelings to free yourself of the torment, which can produce mental and physical stress.

CHRIST IS OUR PERFECT EXAMPLE OF WHAT IT MEANS TO FORGIVE

Resentment is a feeling of hurt or anger because someone threatens your survival. What I am saying here is not just your physical existence but also the emotional "survival" of your self-conception: your opinions, your feelings or the things you identify with your self. During your relationship your mate has, for whatever reason, made you feel belittled, ignored, abandoned, manipulated, committed the wrongful act against your relationship or in other ways attacked you psychologically. You may have a backlog of these painful memories that restrict you and reduce your ability to truly feel free.

Forgiveness is a precept that Christ concerned Himself with to His last breath. "Forgive them, for they know not what they do." His message of love is central to the Christian ethic. Throughout the Gospels, we encounter again and again Christ's pleas for us to love one another and to forgive our trespassers. But there are times even the most sincere Christians (we ministers are not excluded) have their angry and ugly episodes, and for many of them, daily or weekly.

You are not alone. There are times that even those of good intent and strong religious persuasion allow themselves to be angry, bitter, spiteful and resentful. But of all these emotions we experience, for some, the lack of love and forgiveness rears its head more than the others. The longer you hold anger, bitterness, grudges, and resentment inside of you, the more likely those ill emotions will turn into heat and maybe violence. Remember, Christ was hanging on the cross still in pain, suffered many unjustly things by His accusers but He cried out in passion and love, and said Father, forgive them.

Hidden anger and hurt has the power to make your life miserable and often will not go away all on its own. Each time these past or present resentments are reactivated in your mate, your mind and body are subjected to harmful physical and emotional symptoms of stress. These symptoms can cause your muscles to become tense, your thinking to be clouded and your heart may race and your blood pressure could rise. You may mistakenly assume that your anxious feelings are directly caused by the current incident, when in fact the stress—filled reaction in most cases could be caused by the unresolved conflicts with your partner.

Grudge is an ill emotional feeling that comes from not being able to forgive, the longer you hold grudges, the greater the possibility of that ill feeling developing into a more harmful emotion that will cause you to act out inappropriately with your mate. I understand how your wounds from your hurt and pain can sometimes be very deep with some of you, but in this life we learn to receive blows and to forgive those who insult us. As we forgive, it is the beginning of the healing process. Forgiveness is not an act that is always easily done, but the love of Christ and His example of forgiveness is what brings us to that act of love.

Hurt and unresolved conflicts between your partner and you can get hidden away in your subconscious mind for a long time. As far as you are concerned, these feeling have disappeared; you may not be aware that these painful incidents or feelings are affecting your day-to-day experience. Medical science has proven that unresolved hurt and pain that you are holding inside can contribute to serious health problems, such as hypertension, ulcers, heart disease and even cancer.

In the American heritage Dictionary, the word "forgive" means; to excuse for a fault; to pardon. To renounce anger or resentment against the person. To absolve from payment of. To accord forgiveness. In other words, forgive!! A negative attitude toward forgiveness will hold you back from growing as a person, which is crucial to your spirituality and being in right fellowship with God.

As we go through life blaming others for our pain, blame always brings with it anger and anger is a powerful emotion that can get out of control. It very often causes you to act out inappropriately. It can be understandable when you either have or are suffering from the hurt someone may have caused you. You could be terribly hurt, and the pain makes it very difficult to forgive, especially when the person who caused the suffering is the one you trusted the most. But you must understand, forgiveness brings about deliverance and a release to the wounded.

Once you become aware and understand that you may be harboring hidden resentments, the next step is to work through them. This task may not be as easy for some as it is for others. To forgive your partner does not mean that you have to treat him or her like they are someone who never did any wrong. Very simply, to forgive your partner allows you to change your relationship from one of resentment and distrust to one of love. You can disagree with them and still love them very deeply.

You can express your feeling of anger or sadness and not feel alienated from them. In forgiving your mate, you can respect and appreciate the difference and yet learn from them. When a person is holding on to resentment, their past can be a nightmare and the present can be filled with the possibilities for arousing your suppressed anger. Anytime a person goes around holding anger at their mate, they feel ripped by them and possibly by life, and may find themselves constantly trying to get even. Three or more minutes of anger, and you no longer own it, it owns you, and you become its slave.

This person walks around with a chip on their shoulder. They feel that anger is their protection; it is like a roar to scare away adversity. The angry person in a relationship can get angry at the drop of a hat and remembers everything wrong and every injustice he or she has experienced. They are stuck in feelings of anger and blame. This has become a cover-up for their own feelings of inadequacy and hurt. They are just too angry to let go of the hurt and disappointment.

When you forgive your partner and let go of the resentments, your emotions can lighten up. You are no longer defending yourself or are in fear that something or someone will bring up those hurts all over again.

Even if you agree with the importance of forgiveness, there may be a variety of reasons why you have been unable to completely forgive your partner, due to the hurt and painful feeling you are experiencing. For some people, the inability to forgive their partner comes with a desire to feel sorry for themselves and to have a pity party. Still there are others who fail to work through their resentment toward their partner because they insist, "There is nothing wrong, and I have no resentment against my mate or anyone. I am a good person and I am not one who holds grudges." There are so many people who think of themselves as being "nice" and have passed that stage in life that they never have those feelings of resentment.

But so many of us deny that we have no resentment and it keeps us stuck in our misery. When you hold on to animosity, it is like ingesting small doses of poison in your body. Instead of working through your unresolved feelings, there is the possibility of many so-called "nice" people getting headaches, neck pains, ulcers or their buried hurt seeps out little-by-little in acerb comments or bickering. Not only are you putting yourself in physical danger but spiritual danger of falling out of fellowship with Christ. We must forgive that we may be forgiven by Him.

The more you deny these feelings of unforgiveness the more you could be plagued with stress-related symptoms. The reason why so many hurting people sleep may be interrupted, could be from withheld bitterness. This may also be the reason they are experiencing upsetting dreams or why they are having trouble falling asleep in the first place. Many people whose partners are unavailable because of a divorce, or death will pretend the feelings of bitterness have passed, but in reality, they have never really let go of the bitterness.

Then there are some people who simply feel they cannot or will not forgive their partner for unthinkable incidents they remember that are so painful. No matter how much they understand the dangers, physical and spiritual, of carrying around their emotional hurts, they just can't let go. We must keep in mind that Christ who is our perfect example of forgiveness, suffered many unjustly things by His accusers, and afterward, He forgave them in the spirit of love. It is upon us to do the same.

Another point I must make is what most people fail to realize is that by holding on to their resentments, they surrender control over their own emotional well being to the person who hurt them in the first place. In other words, the more they resist letting go of their hurt, the more power they give the resentment and the more the resentment controls their attitude and behavior. By carrying a chip on your shoulder, you may be sacrificing your health and happiness in the vain hope that your persecutor will see how "wrong" they are.

First and foremost, to forgive is the Christ-like way; it is how you regain your emotional freedom, peace of mind and peace with God. But when you are fighting back painful memories, holding the lid on your anger or harboring old resentment, it can affect your relationship in a variety of ways. For instance, if you have unresolved hurt and resentment toward your partner, you may make a subconscious decision that intimacy is dangerous, making you unable to be open and vulnerable in that relationship.

You may be unable to show affection for the people you care about, including your partner or even your children. When you keep your intimate relationships at arm's length and need to stay in complete control in order to feel safe, there is also the possibility of you winding up alone and isolated. Think about it; if we could only learn to forgive and let go resentment, hurt and suppressed disappointment, so many marriages and relationships could be restored.

Sometimes the hardest thing for us to do as Christians is to forgive. The thought of what your mate did to you makes it very difficult to let go. That bad thing he/she did to deceive you when you trusted them so deeply. Now as I am writing this chapter on forgiveness, I must admit that I am no expert on the subject. I only know that I can't live without it. I know that I need the forgiveness of God each day in my life and it is urgent that I not deny it to others.

THE HEALING OF YOUR RESENTMENT

Here is an illustration I use many times when speaking on this very same subject. You can find this in Matt. 18: 23-34. Jesus gives an illustration of a king who decided to bring his accounts up to date. In the process, one of his debtors was brought in to him who owed him approximately $3,000,000. He could not pay it, so the king ordered him to be sold for the debt along with his wife and children and everything he owned. But the debtor fell down before the king, and said, "Oh, king, be patient with me and I will pay it all." Then the king was moved with pity for him and released him and forgave him of his debt.

After the man was forgiven of his debt, he went to a man who owed him approximately $700.00. He grabbed the man by his throat and demanded instant payment. The man fell down before him and begged him to give him a little time. He pleaded with this man and said, "Be patient with me and I will pay it all." But the man would not hear of it. He had him arrested and put in jail until the debt was paid in full.

When this man's friends saw what he had done to the man that owed him, they went back and reported this to the king. The king called this man before him who he had forgiven of his debt and said, "You evil-hearted wretch! I forgave you all of that tremendous debt that you owed me just because you asked me to. Shouldn't you have had mercy on others, just as I had mercy on you? Then the angry king sent the man to the torture chamber until he had paid every last penny due. Jesus tells us so shall our Heavenly Father do unto us if we refuse to truly forgive our brother.

Here are just several examples that should be an encouragement to recognize His willingness to forgive us of our wrong:

The woman caught in adultery	John 8: 3-11.
The woman who anointed Christ feet with oil	Luke 7: 47-50.
Peter, for denying he knew Jesus	John 18: 15-18, 25-27,21: 15-19

The thief on the cross   Luke 23:39-43.

The people who crucified Him   Luke 23:34.

Learning to forgive from our heart had been advocated and demonstrated by our greatest spiritual and religious teacher of all, Jesus Christ Himself. As Christians, we are called to forgive. It is a part of our spiritual DNA that connects us with Christ who is our source.

Forgiveness is the one gift we most need, both to give and receive. Each time we forgive, it is a healing as God's love flows through us. Forgiveness is made possible by the forgiveness extended to us in Jesus Christ. When we refuse to forgive others, we are then setting ourselves above the ultimate sacrifice of Christ.

CHAPTER 7

WHY SHOULD YOU BUY THE COW WHEN YOU ARE GETTING THE MILK FOR FREE?

The word "Shacking-up" is a word, which describes an immoral relationship of any couple that lives together as though they were married.

Living together outside of marriage was once considered by most bad and immoral. But in these last days it has become so common that if you tell your parents you are going to move in with your significant other, they probably roll their eyes and say pass the peas please. The number of opposite couples living together jumped 13% from about 8%) to 7.5 millions according to the Census Bureau Demographers. According to their report, you can blame the sluggish job market, which has forced many young adults to share living quarters.

Broader societal issues are at work. Researchers estimate that more than half of married couples live together before they get married. Only 38% of Americans believe that unmarried couples living together is bad for society; half said it doesn't make much difference according to a Rew Research center

Survey. Young adults along with older adults, who have been married, view living together as a way to avoid the hassles often associated with the end of a marriage. But if you and your partner share property, a break-up could be messier than a dish-throwing divorce.

I find that there are many questions concerning the subject of marriage and shacking-up. Hear are a few to start with: Why should we worry about getting marriage when we are happy already? What difference does a piece of paper make? Who needs a wedding? Do you not know that Black Women are the least likely in our society to get married? One just might ask you sister, could it be that you are getting played. And maybe you should ask yourself, what kind of a woman am I?

In a research study it shows a most frequent reason given by women for living together was that they were looking forward to marriage. The males verbalized their motives as "sexual convenience and pleasure." One in the study stated, " if you're living with a lady, it's a lot easier to get your way with her!"

Another study revealed that the most common complaint of live-in by women is: "I sometimes get the feeling I am being used." It doesn't take some of the young ladies long to figure out how the male attitude is toward marriage. Another male stated in the study; "why should I risk marriage when I can get everything I need without tying myself down to a lifelong commitment and responsibility?"

So many of these young ladies have their own apartment or home. But often they are being manipulated by their male partners through deceptive measures of false promises just to move in with them but avoiding the commitment of marriage and the responsibility that goes along with the commitment. Most of these young men have no job nor are they searching for one. And if we are allowed to be real, it has nothing to do with the sluggish job market.

There are too many of our young women who are so desperate for a relationship that they allow non working brothers to move in with them, even if he does not get a job or marry her. Many times they both know it is not a match from the beginning. But she hangs in with him anyway; trying against all odds to make it work or hoping she will be able to change him.

And so it is with so many of our young ladies in today's society. They become so desperate and needy that they feel it is necessary for them to lower their Godly standards to have a mate. There is a young lady I have known for many years, she had a very good job that paid her well for her professional ability. This young lady had her own home and a nice car. But she was lonely for a man to be in her life, so it was not too hard to settle with the idea of lowing her standards, she felt that it would be the only way she could get a mate.

She concluded with the existing thought in her mind, "after all I am a large size girl and I can't be to choosy," so she called up this guy who had been trying to get a date with her for a while. (1) It was discovered he lives with his mother. She is moving into denial, "Well he did ask me out for dinner, I see no wrong in that." (2) The very next night she goes over to pick him up, why? The brother has no car to go and pick her up. She said to herself, "I can understand he is trying to get back on his feet." (3) After dinner, comes time to pay the bill, guess what? (4) He said to her, "Baby I hope you can understand my circumstances, I was in the system for six months on some false charges. I am working now but they have not paid me yet, can you take care of this?" How does she respond? The lady pays the $63.43 bill, that's how she responded (5) Big mistake. She takes him to her house on their first date, just to be sociable and see a movie. She is now fully in denial. She says to herself, "Because I don't want him to think I am one of those sister's who don't understand or, I am afraid to trust him because he has been in jail." After watching an R rated movie, it was very late and it is time to take him home. (6) He is now getting ready to play her, to see just how weak she is before making his final move. "Baby how about letting me stay over tonight and sleep on your sofa? It is very late, I will have to wake my mother, and she is sick and not feeling well." Well, after thinking it over she thought to herself, "What harm could it be to let him stay over? It is the weekend and I don't have to go to work tomorrow. He had been nice the whole time we have been together, and it will be nice to have a man here to fix breakfast for tomorrow, then I will take him home."

The one night stay over became a week, (7) and one week . . . you are right!! The brother has now moved in. The sister is now in complete denial. Five months later he still has no job, (8) She reassures herself, "He is trying, and they just don't want to give him a chance because he has been in jail. I even let him take me to work so he can use the car everyday to look for work." After being chased by the police, he crashed her car into a tree. She said, "They say that they have been watching him for months and he had drugs on him, they are lying he doesn't use drugs, they are only messing with him because he is black and has a record."

I have no good news to give you on this young lady and her man. It is because my last meeting with him and her sometime ago, they are still together. The jail and correctional system has become a revolving door for this young man. It seems as though he has conditioned himself in the exceptive of the correctional system as a way of life. And the young lady? She is still in denial, while being used and being taken advantage of by her man. She says, "I know he loves me, we are just going through some hard times right now, but he said things are going to get better." Because of her man's irresponsibility and troubles, she no longer has that nice home or that nice car, she also lost that good paying job that she once enjoyed. This young lady and her man had to move in with her mother for a while; but she and he now have an apartment and they are both living off of her new low paying job. There is a quote I want to give to the ladies who compromise their standards and values. "When you compromise yourself, you have to practice not looking embarrassed." I believe that God has a mate for everyone who desires one according to His will. You don't have to compromise yourself.

A SPECIAL NOTE TO THE LADIES;

Don't expect your man to get a job, and taking responsibility by putting a ring on your finger and marry you when he is living comfortably in your house, eating your food, driving your car and spending your money as you lay with your legs open being available sexually for him to relieve himself in. Baby-girl, set some standards for yourself and your relationship, he cannot respect you when you have no respect for yourself. "Why should he buy the cow, when all he is getting or could want is **free**?"

A SPECIAL NOTE TO THE MOTHERS;

Mothers, make sure you are not raising up your sons to be your man. When you have no life of your own but are all up in his marriage and his relationships with his women and you refuse to let him go. Something is wrong with this picture. You are secretly and subconsciously thinking that he is your man. He is not your man!! He is your son. Mothers, you must get on with your own life and release your son and let him go. So your son can learn how to become a man, and taking the responsibility in providing care and support for the babies he has produced while not rejecting the responsibilities of fatherhood.

Marriage and the responsibility that goes with it gives a couple the opportunity for happiness, although for the most part it does not provide them with the wherewithal to achieve it. There is no magic in the wedding itself to change people or circumstances. There is no love potion that guarantees the couple will live together "happily ever after." No words spoken on the wedding day can really teach the couple how to achieve lasting bliss. Whatever happiness they achieve will result from personal effort, knowledge, love, commitment and responsibility. The wedding makes few internal changes, but it does make dramatic changes in status, rights, and opportunities. Live-in lovers might find it possible to avoid divorce lawyers and sometime alimony, but often there are no fewer tears, heartaches, disappointments or problems.

As a pastor I must be truthful with you, and this truth is based on the teachings of Biblical principles. The Bible advocates marriage between a man and woman, not "shacking-up" and I cannot teach any other alternative. You have the choice to live the lifestyle you wish to live. I have chosen to live my lifestyle as I do, to preach and teach Biblical principles in accordance with the word of God, including marriage. This is what makes me feel right. People look for the preacher to validate their wrongdoings and wrong actions. They are looking for the preacher to give them a comfort zone that supports their wrong and their immoral actions. As spiritual leaders, we will not and should not give them a plan for failure.

WHY CAN'T IT BE ME WHO IS MARRIED? I AM DESPERATE, CAN'T WAIT ANY LONGER.

You are tired of coming home alone, it seems like there is no one out there for you. When you come from church, from the movies, from work, or from a night out alone for dinner you end up at home all by yourself. You don't want to be branded as a desperate lonely person who is in need of a mate, but in reality this is how you are feeling. You are tired of sleeping all by yourself. Why can't it be you who is married; you are running out of patience, you now find yourself examining the possibility of lowering your standards and morals to settle for less, saying to yourself, "if he/she has two matching shoes, I'll take them."

Nothing you have done so far has enabled you to hook-up with a soul mate. You have tried everything; the Internet, singles groups at church, and networking parties.

Nothing has worked for your personal needs. In your heart you know that God does not want you to be alone, but your loneliness sometimes causes you to feel doubtful. You try to cope with your singleness; you ask," Is there anyone out there for me?"

I find that when so many people are in desperate need of a soul mate for a prolonged period of time, often they begin to feel hopeless. Some yield to the temptation to grow bitter with themselves and others. The question is who would want to have a relationship with a bitter person? But many people do become bitter, angry and frustrated. They lose their faith and their self-esteem.

So it was in the case of a young lady that I have known for many years. She was then as she is now a very beautiful and attractive woman. Lets' call her Anita. She is the mother of four children. Anita has been in all three of her sisters' weddings, one of which I was the officiating minister. Anita and her sisters have always been very close, like a Brat Pack. These four sisters would always go out together to movies, dinners and parties. They all attended the same church and have always had a wonderful social life.

As much as each of them enjoyed being together, they would always hope and pray for their continual happiness and that one-day they all would be happily married. Anita gave the bridal shower for each of the sisters and gave the bachelorette party; she was a maid of honor in each of the sisters' weddings.

If you were allowed to go into Anita's bedroom and open her closet door you would see the beautiful dresses all in different styles and colors. As beautiful as these dresses are they are also a painful reminder to this young lady that she is still lonely with absolutely no one in her life to marry her. To add insult to injury, Anita's youngest brother is getting married and she is asked to be in that wedding. It seems like everyone around her was getting married, her self-esteem was low, and she started feeling hopeless.

Because of Anita's desperation to be married and have a father for the kids, many men have been in and out of her life. The desperation resulted in her lowering her standards to try and find a man who would love and marry her. This young lady needed the love and care of a mate, so she gave sex to get love but even in that something was missing. The loneliness and un-fulfillment was still there. There were two or more times she thought that she had finally found someone, but as it was with all the others they were not ready for marriage.

She told me of this one man even though she felt that he was using her, she still cared a lot for him. She had asked him; "Why won't you marry me? My children love you and they need a father and I need a husband. We have been going together for a long time, why can't we get married?" He answered: "Now why would you want to mess up a good thing?" He said, "This is not the time to be talking about that, you don't just hurry and jump into things like marriage." She said to him; "You always come here and in a hurry to jump in bed with me to have sex, we should not be doing that but you are not complaining. What if I stop having sex with you until you marry me, will you still love me?"

The more Anita would talk about the frustration and bitterness that had built up inside her from being used by men, the more emotionally and tearful she became. She told me the painful story of her oldest daughter feeling it was her responsibility to care for the one sister and two brothers, even as a little girl (although they are only a year apart) when she saw mommy and boyfriend go into the bedroom. She stated; "I am so shameful of the nature of my behavior which has caused so much emotional pain not only on myself but most of all, my children. They have experienced the shameful feeling of their mother living this immoral life before them. My desperation for a husband blinded me morally, which allowed me to try and build a marriage by having sex with men. I am so ashamed of myself and the hurt and disappointment I put my children through."

Anita shared with me her feelings of sadness and regrets and said; "All of the men that have ever been in my life were only taking advantage of my vulnerability." She said, "There was this one man I so desperately tried to build a lasting relationship with, but he would become withdrawn anytime I would bring up the subject of marriage." She expressed the sadness in her heart and the disappointment for allowing herself to be so emotionally vulnerable and sexually abused by these men, who only viewed her as a sexual partner and nothing more. They had no desire to have a future with her. Anita made herself available (the milk was free) sexually for these men to relieve themselves.

When you are trying to fill an empty space with empty actions, in the end, you are left alone feeling sad and disappointed. It is not good for you to try to do that which is immoral out of hurt and desperation, giving sex to get love is un-fulfillment. The receiver gives love only for a moment just to get sex. You must realize within yourself that you are too beautiful and valuable to allow yourself to be played over, or to minimize your importance to be taken advantage off.

Anita told me about a man whom she allowed to live with her and her kids, for a long period of time although she felt he was cheating in the relationship. Her desperation for a husband and vulnerability resulted in her becoming adjusted to his behavior. She recalled talking to him on the subject of marriage: "You have told me over and over that one day we would sit down and discuss marriage, now is the time, I want to get marriage." He replied by saying; "Girl you are crazy, why would I be thinking about marriage now? This is not the time for that." Anita responded by saying; "I am getting tired of living this way, this is not right and I am setting a bad example for my children, I am ashamed of myself and this is immoral." He answered by saying; "Your children are fine the way things are, you need to get that mess out of your head. I have something I need to tell you anyway, I am going out of town for a while on a new job and I am not sure when I will be back."

This desperate young lady, who has experienced the disappointment and rejection from one relationship to another, was devastated. I was told of the betrayal and deceitfulness of the live-in man whom she discovered one Saturday afternoon was cheating on her. Anita had taken the children to the park for some playtime. While the children were playing she was sitting on the bench trying to get ahead on some overdue reading. Not too long afterward she noticed her live-in boyfriend, who was supposed to be out of town working, had pulled up to the park in his car with a young lady and two kids. After they had gotten out of the car, he saw Anita sitting on the bench nearby reading a book and he immediately said to the mystery woman, "Let's go to the other side of the park, I like it over there better?" As soon as Anita heard her live-in man's voice she turn and saw him, as he and the mystery woman and kids was going back to the car, he gave Anita a pleading signal not to blow his cover. She embarrassingly told me; "I complied with his wishes, so like a good girl I became the faded person in the background of the picture."

At this point I was waiting to hear Anita express the anger and resentfulness she held against this man for the way he had taken advantage of her weakness and immoral state, and his lying and using her for his satisfaction. I was surprised, this young lady was a renewed individual she said; "You know Elder Johnson, I allowed my desperation for a man to cause me to down graded myself importance and character and to be taken advantage off, I am better than that it was like a light had popped on in my head. That experience was a defining moment for me, I was free!! And I had no animosity against anyone. I was able to forgive myself. I have asked God to forgive me for my foolishness and wrongful behavior, how I conducted myself before my children, and my children who are now young adults have also forgiven me and they love me.

I have not returned into the world nor have I fallen back into any sinful relationships. I was foolishly jeopardizing my health and well-being. My foolish emphatic behavior could have resulted in a sexual transmitted disease. I foolishly put myself at risk being involved in premarital sex with different partners. I am happy to say, I am no longer bitter or angry and I am forgiven. There has been an inspirational renewal in my spirit; thanks to you Elder Johnson and most of all thanks to God, I am better. I am now trusting in God and allowing Him to mold me into a woman of integrity with the right attitude toward relationships. I now realize what you were trying to get me to understand when you told me more than once that: "if I would keep my attitude regarding relationships Godly, then my desires will be the ones God would honor."

In spite of all the statistics, the ratio of women to men in every city is 3 to 1, there are a number of men who are disqualified as mates because they are either in jail, gay, hooked on drugs, drug pushers, or not saved. Then you have the number of men who do not choose women of your color, your body type, or your educational level and so forth. I am sure if you are looking for a mate, you have heard these discouraging statistics. All of these discouraging odds can make those of you who are waiting and expecting "Mr./Ms. Right" to feel disoriented and hopeless in ever finding your soul mate.

But if you read the verses in Psalm 37, which contain promises from God that makes perfect sense in trusting and waiting. As we allow the process of trusting and waiting to perfect us, it is actually molding our desires to God's will for our life. God becomes our delight during this process, and our view of marriage becomes synonymous with His views. You cannot marry a person out of emotions; if this is what you are counting on to give you happiness and peace in marriage you have no true foundation to build your marriage upon.

There are those who are living immoral lives everyday by shacking-up, engaged in premarital sex and having the boldness to tell you; "I know that I am saved." ***What they don't understand is that none can be saved if they refuse to line up their life with the word of God.*** The Bible clearly tells us; "For this is the will of God, even your sanctification, that ye should abstain from fornication.1Thess. 4:3. (kjv). Just to add to it, none of us has the right to live immoral lives. Although you do have the choice to live as you choose, you also are held accountable for the choice you make.

I would like to offer these words from the Bible; "Then shall the dust return to the earth as it was: And the spirit return unto God who gave it." Ecclesiastes 12:7. (kjv). Death is a common lot of us all, that no one can escape, and what we all must understand is; "that there is life after death." The Bible tells us that we all shall stand before the judgment seat of God, to give an account of our deeds. There is no way of getting around it. Here is what the Bible says in Ecclesiastes 12:14. "For God shall bring every work into judgment, with every secret thing, whether it be good, or whether it be evil." (kjv).

A word to the wise, you who are shacking together and doing other wrong and un-Godly things that you think no one knows about, you are deceiving yourselves, God knows. He also knows about you who are married and slipping around having extramarital affairs, be it husband or wife, God knows; and often we are fooling ourselves to think that people don't know.

DYSFUNCTIONAL AND ABUSED ENVIRONMENT; SHE HAS LOW SELF-ESTEEM, HOW?

There are a lot of people with low self-esteem. Many of them are that way, because of the message and treatment they have been receiving: "I wish you had never been born." "I think they made a mistake in the hospital, you could not be my child." "Your face is too black, you are too ugly." "Why can't you be like somebody else? "You stupid fool!! You can never do anything right." "Why don't you crawl in a hole and die."

If you dig a hole in front of people, the only thing they can do is crawl into the hole. If you put a pedestal in front of people and give them encouragement, they will eventually get up on the pedestal and feel good about themselves. If ten, twenty, and thirty years of negative tap, tap, taps are the only things they hear, how can a person feel good about themselves and be happy?

The only way people can get out of that hole is through unconditional love, and they will start experiencing it from the people around them as soon as they start to take positive action. In unconditional love there is no ill treatment. The greatest power we all have in our lives is the power to love. Love is a decision we make in our lives that says others are as important as we are and we will make a commitment to their happiness, development, and security, to the same level, as we would do for ourselves.

When the parent response is always negative to their child, they are emotionally wounded through the failure of their parents whose responsibility it is to provide emotional safety. When they fail to respond to their child for their efforts in a positive way, there is an interruption in positive growth and development in the life of their child. Their child experiences a physiological let down and views this as being his or her own "fault." Not all parents are capable of responding to their children in a "good enough" manner.

I recall back during the time when I was in my pre-teens, there was a lady who lived down the street from where we lived. This lady had only one child by birth, a girl, (let's call her Jean) who was the same age as my sisters, which was a year younger than I. When Jean could get away from home (which was not that often) she would always come to our house to play with my sisters. Jean was a very nice girl and very smart in school, but she was always a lonely child with very low self-esteem, the product and result of ill treatment she received from her mother on a daily basis, (let's call her Ms. John.). Ms. John had taken in a girl (let's call her Marie) who was very beautiful, her hair was long and silky, she was half white what we as kids would called them back then "mixed." Ms. John's own daughter was dark skinned, with short and very nappy hair. Ms. John would always take Marie into town on the weekend with her and buy her nice clothes and other things she would desire, while Jean, her child by birth would only receive hand-me-down clothes Ms. John could no longer wear. Sometimes my mother would make nice dresses and other clothes for Jean to wear to school, because her mother didn't provide any for her.

Ms. John loved Marie very much and there was nothing she would not do for that girl. But her own child "Jean" by birth, she hated her. "You are so black, you is a dam ugly." "I wish you were dead." Often these are the words or similar negative words, which identify Jean as the daughter Ms. John. While Ms. John was always sitting, combing and playing in Marie's fine hair, she would make Jean wash the dishes, clean the house, wash the clothes and hang them out on the line to dry. After the clothes have dried she must now go out and bring them in and put them up. Ms. John treated her child like, for lack of a better word, "nothing.' It seem that the lady was punishing her own daughter for being born. I later learned in life that Ms. John carried the burden of her own history of deprivation and neglect, and often Jean suffered the consequences of the mother's dysfunctional disturbers.

Ms. John sometimes would beat Jean so bad that we would cry for her. Many times Jean would run down to our house into my mother's arms for safety. My mother often begged Ms. John to "Please let me keep Jean here with my children, I will take good care of her for you. If you keep beating this child like this you are going to kill her." Many times when my mother heard that Ms. John was abusing Jean, she would go to her house and get Jean and bring her to our house to stay with us until the rage of her mother had ended. When my mother was allowed to, she would go by and get Jean and take her to church with us on Sundays. Jean really love going to church with us, and staying over one or two nights when she could. Two or three days later Ms. John will come get Jean and take her back to her house. Although we were just kids at the time, I am sorry to say this but we did not like that lady.

I recalled so many times in school, boys would be back in the gym where no one could see them and they would force Jean to have sex with them. This girl was so emotionally and physiologically wounded and craved for love so bad, she would allow herself to be used by boys at school just to have someone to hold her in their arms. There was this one boy that she really cared about but he did not care anything for her, none of them did. This boy would use her and then make fun of her afterward. There would be times this same boy would be so low to tell Jean "If you love me, then after you give me some, you have to give my two friends some." She would do it just to please him; she would feel that it is her "fault" if this person would no longer love her.

This girl thought very little of herself, never being told by her mother or hearing the words "I love you." "You are a very smart girl." (She was very smart) "Thank you for cleaning the house." "You are getting very good grades in school, I am so proud of you." Jean craved for love so desperately, but resolved within herself that she was not worthy of ever finding true love. I remember the time my sisters were trying to discourage Jean from allowing guys to use her sexually, Jean told them; " It don't matter to me that much, they give me love. And I give them sex just to pretend to myself for that moment that I am special and I'm being loved by someone who really needs me, I feel bad when it is all over knowing they don't really want me, sometime I feel so empty inside but that's alright."

At the age of fourteen Jean was found dead, tied to a tree. Some white men had raped her and left her there tied to that tree to die. Jean's mother told everyone, including the police officers that this evil deed was done by the same white men (who were never arrested) who raped her several times before as she would be walking home from the store, but as you know back then, and in the State of

Mississippi!! Like so many others of their kind, those white men were ever arrested for the senseless act and crime they had committed.

FOR YOUR CONSIDERATION:

If you don't like yourself, you can't be happy and pleased with who you are as a person. I believe that positive self-worth is the essential requirement for self-appreciation. Unless we accept ourselves as we are, we will spend our lives trying to prove ourselves that we are worthwhile by actions that will leave us feeling empty, and in relationships that are doomed to failure.

In our communities we are seeing more and more single-mother households, we are seeing a number of young people who don't even have relationships with their fathers, and the sadness to this, most of them don't know who their father is. During slavery a black child was more likely to grow up with both parents than he or she is today. You could say that one of the reasons such facts stand out so, is we as a whole have not effectively dealt with the relationship between Black men and women.

We must reach out to our young black men and teach them how to deal with the process of making good choices in relationships and commitment. Teaching them what manhood is, because if we continue to allow our young to define manhood as sexual prowess and machismo, then we are going to continue to see more single mothers and more of our males in jail. It is reported that in 1980, 1 in 3 black males were involved in the penal system. In 2007 1 in 3 are involved. It is projected that in 2020, 2 in 3 black males will be in the penal system.

That being said, these projections gives raise, reasons and the importance why we as black men should do a better job in providing good examples of what it is to be a real man. As real men we understand that at the end of the day, what will define us most is what they leave to the next generation, not what they have accumulated for themselves.

Parents should enroll their male child in a rite-of-passage program; the Boy Scouts is a good program for them to start. Our boys need to be exposed to etiquette, chivalry, math, more reading, power, sex education, the arts, as well as athleticism. Our girls should be enrolled in a rite-of-passage program; there must be more of our girls exposed to etiquette, reading, math, the arts, and sex education. It is so important that our girls also learn self worth and positive body reinforcement as well as learning to love and respect themselves first.

Self-worth is when we have the ability to say, "I am a good and well founded person." This is something we must believe with all of our heart. As we live by the high morals and Godly standards we have set for ourselves. In accepting ourselves, we are to set aside any need to impress others or to win their validation as to who we are as a person. We are to live at a level of comfort in which we can really be ourselves. One of the greatest luxuries in life is the freedom to be ourselves, and to know we are wonderful people just the way we are.

In this life we should see our own goodness, appreciate our assets and abilities, and celebrate our self worth as a person who is wonderfully made by God. We should acknowledge our differences and uniqueness from other people. We are one of a kind, who is special. If we live to please others to win their validation and approval of ourselves and who we are as a person, if we do things we really don't want to do, if we go against our true feeling or conscience, the actions and outcomes will leave us feeling negative about ourselves and unfulfilled. Our actions are who we are, so "to thine own self be true."

CHAPTER 8

CONTENTMENT AND FORGIVENESS, IN RELATIONSHIPS.

"Not that I speak in respect of want: I have learned, in whatever state I am, therefore to be content. I know both how to be abased (in need), and I know how to abound (have plenty): everywhere and in all things I am instructed both to be full and to be hungry, both to abound and suffer need. I can do all things through Christ, which strengthened me." Phil.4: 11-13. (kjv.)

Are you content in any circumstances you face? True contentment comes from one's inner faith; one who is able to reside in his circumstances and build upon his strength from within unto the glory of the Lord. Although Paul was writing from prison, to the saints at Philippi, joy was the dominant theme in his letter. Here his writing encourages us. Paul says "I have learned the secret that whatever state I am in to be content." We can have joy, even in hardship. What we must understand is that joy does not come from outward circumstances but from our inward strength of faith in Jesus Christ. Being grounded in the word of God we can have profound contentment, serenity, and peace of mind no matter what happens.

Each day we should be encouraged, showing the glory of God in our lives, instead of complaining. This joy comes from knowing Christ personally, having our own personal experience in Him and depending on His strength rather than our own. As blood washed believers, we must not rely on what we have or what we experience to give us joy, but on Jesus Christ who is within us.

People today desperately want to be happy in their living but are tossed and turned by daily situations, failures, and inconveniences. Often in our lives we go through trials, tribulations and setbacks. There are times the circumstances we undergo will have us to look back over our life and see that we have not made as much progress as we desire. The unfavorable results of these situations cause some to fall into spiritual depression being immersed in their fears and failures. The disappointment will have you complaining, worrying and deprived of your courage and confidence. Every apparent setback is only temporary and in the reality of our faith, it is only a set up for a better tomorrow if we could only see it that way. In Christ we can be joyful in every circumstance, even when things are going badly, even when we feel like complaining, even when no one else is there to encourage us.

When we come to Christ we are surrendering ourselves to Him. In essence you are turning yourself over to God for His use. We come to understand that life is not going to be easy or better. You won't go through life with a plastic, frozen smile because God's going to put you on a magic carpet and let you float through life without experiencing some things other people experience. The Bible says that God allows some rain to fall on the just and the unjust alike. You're going to experience things in life everybody else experiences. The difference is that you're going to have the assurance of knowing who you are, where you've come from, what you're doing, who you belong to, and where you're going to end up.

Pain is a part of life, part of the human equation. We all will experience some pain, be it physical, mental, emotional, or spiritual. To expect life to be pain free is to deny humanness. Most of us never learn from pain. We experience these painful situations and are so relieved when they are over, we never look at it to define a teachable moment. We learn our greatest lessons about ourselves, and life from not only facing painful situations but also examining the pain. Through pain, we define who we are. A painful situation is an opportunity to grow.

In the midst of these painful situations, God can birth new blessings and beginnings. As a couple you must stand united against Satan when he attacks your relationship, and remember, the greater your faith is in the Lord, the greater the power of authority is in you against the assignments of Satan that will come against you. Knowing when adversities attack, defines the character of your relationship.

LETTING GO OF RESENTMENT

Often we obstruct our relationships by stockpiling resentment toward our mate. This resentment becomes a lethal arsenal of anger, hatred and disdain that ignites instantly whenever a problem arises between you and your mate. Resentment and the anger that underlies it blocks the flow of caring for one another, it inhibits a resolution of the problem, denies the possibility of mature love, and can damage your physical health and well-being. It is also impossible to recognize the fullness of our lives when we are angry and resentful. Releasing such resentment is the first crucial step of the love renewal process.

If we can learn to forgive one another, release from our inner torment of anger is possible. Ironically, the refusal to forgive is the ultimate cause of resentment, and the true victim of resentment is always the one who refuses to forgive. The two concepts of resentment and forgiveness are distinctly similar in that neither is a feeling. Both of these concepts are willful choices that lead to decisive actions. We make a choice to be resentful or to forgive. Yet resentment drives us away from one another, while forgiveness draws us toward each other to commitment.

Forgiving is not synonymous with forgetting. When we forgive, we accept character flaws, differences of opinion, and separate identities, as well as the inevitable frustrations and disappointment that accompany situations that do not go according to plan. When we forgive, we arrive to work things out. We share our feelings, we share our thoughts, and we share our solutions. When two people are in a relationship, there is a connection that brings about relevance one to another.

Forgetting has a very different outcome of the situation. When we forget, we reject our mate. We ignore them. We refuse to communicate, eat or even sleep with her/him.

Instead, we choose our work, TV, friends, other things and the love of other people. Rather than work things out, we leave. We don't just forget the issues; we tend to forget the whole person. We try to block out our feelings, as well as repressing our thoughts, and we seldom reach any solutions. To release yourself from the inner torment of anger, resentment and the bitterness, you must be willing to forgive. From the Holy Bible, Jesus gives us this requirement that you may have peace from within and with the Father; "And when ye stand praying, forgive, if ye have ought against any: that your Father also which is in heaven may forgive you your trespasses. But if ye not forgive, neither will your Father which is in heaven forgive your trespasses." (Mark 11: 25-26).

We must forgive if we are to love maturely. This process is ongoing, requires continual communication and must become a daily part of our lives. Many people will warehouse their resentment for years before cashing them in, usually by dumping a huge pile of bitterness and complaints. Harboring resentment seems only too natural, but there is a better way. All we need is the courage to talk with one another. Yet this basic requirement is surprisingly painful for many people. Talking about your resentment to your mate is not easy, but learning how to communicate with your mate is a crucial point in the renewal process. Communication in some ways is so integrally related to intimacy that even the sharing of your negative resentment could bring you closer together.

So don't be discouraged by your hurt and anger. Your feelings of bitterness will go away. It may not seem that way when you are upset but they do. You may be so discouraged by your negative feelings that you have very little confidence that this can help but give it a try. Don't let your present anger get in the way of you having peace in your relationship. When you are angry, the future looks bleak and happy moments of the past cannot be remembered. When your anger subsides, your mood will improve. So will your memory! Research has clearly shown that people remember far fewer pleasant events when they are upset. Once your anger and hurt diminish, you and your mate will be able to work through the more enduring resentments that trigger these ill feelings over and over again.

I am reminded of a story I read from a book a few years ago, I can't remember the title of the book nor can I remember the author who had written it. In one of the chapters of that book the writer tells of an interesting story about a person who gives an account of an earlier event and the lesson learned when they were young. Here is the story as best as I can remember: "When I was a little kid, my mom liked to make breakfast food for dinner every now and then. I remember one night in particular when she made breakfast after a hard days work. On that evening so long ago, my mom placed a plate of eggs, sausage and extremely burned biscuits in front of my dad. I remember waiting to see if anyone noticed! Yet all my dad did was reach for his biscuit, smile at my mom and ask me how my day was at school. I don't remember what I told him that night, but I do remember watching him smear butter and jelly on that biscuit and bite! When I got up from the table that evening, I remember hearing my mom apologize to my dad for burning the biscuits. And I'll never forget what he said" "Honey, I love burned biscuits."

"Later that night, I went to kiss my daddy good night and I asked him if he really liked his biscuits burned. He wrapped me in his arms and said, "Your momma put in a hard day at work today and she's real tired. Besides a little burnt biscuit never hurt anyone!"

Life is full of imperfect things, and imperfect people. I'm not the best at hardly anything, and just as so many others do sometimes, I forget birthdays and anniversaries. But what I've learned over the years is that learning to accept each others faults and choosing to celebrate each others differences is one of the most important keys to creating a healthy, growing and lasting relationship.

It is my hope and prayer that if you are experiencing some unfavorable circumstances in your life or within your relationship, you would learn to take the good, the bad, and the ugly parts of your life and lay them at the feet of Jesus. In the end, He's the only one who will be able to give you the kind of relationship where a burnt biscuit of life isn't a deal-breaker.

I can recall complaining to my mother when I was a little boy about how upset I was because I did not get everything I wanted for Christmas that year. I recall her saying to me "Son, we must learn to adapt to situations in life, we may not always get all we want or wish to have in life so we adjust to the situation." A lesson learned! So we adjust to the situation and we affirm ourselves for growth, then we are able to move more soundly toward our destiny when we adapt to our circumstances in life. In fact, understanding is the base of any relationship, be it a husband-wife or parent-child or friendship. Someone told me many years ago that "You don't put the key to your happiness in someone else's pocket, keep it in your own."

SOME THINGS YOU SHOULD UNDERSTAND ABOUT ANGER

1. Anger will not help you to think clearly enough to find a peaceful solution to your problem. If there is a solution to your situation, the anger and resentment will keep you from finding it.

2. Angry thoughts often involve issues of fairness. If you learn to look at things through other people's eyes, sometimes you will find that their actions are not unfair, from their perspective.

3. Angry thoughts nearly always contain distortions. By correcting these distortions it will reduce your anger.

4. Getting even seldom gets you what you want. It usually provokes counterattack or withdrawal.

5. Accepting the idea that you are responsible for your anger is ultimately to your advantage, because it gives you the opportunity to achieve control and change how you feel.

6. Letting go of anger gets you closer to love, if this is what you truly desire.

Anger will hold you back from having a spirit that is pleasing to God; therefore we should resolve our problems as soon as possible. Jesus said this in Matt. 5: 23-24. "Therefore if thou bring thy gift to the altar, and there remembers that thy brother hath ought against thee; leave there thy gift before the altar, and go thy way; first be reconciled to thy brother, and then come and offer thy gift." It is very hypocritical to say we love God while we hate or cannot forgive others. The word of God is clear on this: our attitude toward others reflects the kind of relationship we have with Him.

Anger is a dangerous emotion that threatens to spring out of control. The longer we hold anger, grudges, bitterness, and resentfulness inside of us, the more likely that these ill feelings will turn into hate and maybe to violence. Emotional hurt can increase mental stress and broken relationships and can result in a violation of God's commandment to love. The test of our love for God is in how we treat others in response to how they have wronged us. It is understandable not to love the wrong behaviors of the person but we are to have a Christ love for them and to forgive them of their wrong that we may also be forgiven.

Through careful communication, couples can be reconciled. Commitment can be renewed and romance refreshed. Don't let walls come between you and your mate. Couples should always try and take care of problems while they are still small.

Our love for our spouse makes them appear beautiful. It is the inner qualities that keep love alive. Don't just look for physical attractiveness in a spouse. Look for the qualities that don't fade with time. One should look for qualities that are sound such as these: Spiritual commitment, integrity, sensitivity and sincerity.

So often people go into a relationship expecting everything to be all happy and a bed of roses, because they are so gratified and filled with satisfaction. They have found that special person in their lives who has filled their life with joy and happiness. That special person who likes the same things, have the same qualities in common and have similar traits. They are so joyous that all is well and their relationship is full of life with blue skies, not realizing that in everyone's life some rain must fall.

Those who go into a relationship or marriage expecting only sunny days and blue skies absent from all stormy clouds and rain, have not really prepared themselves for the commitment of that relationship or marriage. No matter how compatible the couple may be, having the same qualities and similar traits they are two different people. Being two different people, especially man and woman, their behavior is not the same. Figuratively speaking, they are from two different planets.

> *The words we speak in anger*
> *can heal or be destructive.*

So many relationships are destroyed due to an uncontrolled tongue. A few destructive words spoken in anger can destroy a relationship that took years to build. So before you speak, you should realize that wrong words are like fire and you can neither control nor reverse (call back) the damage they do.

Damaging words can spread quickly and you cannot stop the consequences once they are spoken. To seek forgiveness later for the wrong you have caused will not remove the destruction that has been done. We sometimes say words out of hurt or anger in hopes of making ourselves feel better not realizing we are making a bigger mess of the situation. Know that words used in the wrong way can pull a person down; they can destroy and, yes, even cause a death. Think before you speak. Ask yourself: is this what I truly want to say? Is it necessary? Is it kind?

Below are some lead-in phrases that may help you to express your feelings of anger, sadness, fear, regret and love to your mate. The point here is to communicate to your mate in a more loving and caring way. To do this in a more appropriate and caring fashion, give yourself time to release the intensity of angry and negative thoughts. These lead-in phrases may not work for everyone or in every situation that comes up but the key point is to communicate, as difficult as it may be, in a loving and forgiving way, to restore your relationship.

1. <u>For anger:</u> **I don't like it when . . . I feel frustrated that/whenI am angry that . . . I feel annoyed when . . . I want . . .**
2. <u>For sadness:</u> **I feel disappointed . . . I am sad . . . I feel hurt I wanted . . . / I want . . .**
3. <u>For fear:</u> **I feel worried . . . I am afraid . . . I feel scared . . . I do not want . . . / I need . . . . I want . . .**
4. <u>For regret:</u> **I feel embarrassed . . . I am sorry . . . I feel ashamed . . . I didn't want . . . I want . . .**
5. <u>For love:</u> **I love . . . I want . . . I understand . . . I forgive . . . I appreciate . . . I thank you for . . . I know . . .**

To expect communication to always be easy is unrealistic. Some feelings are very difficult to communicate without hurting your mate. Couples who have wonderful and loving relationships will sometimes agonize over how to communicate in a way that works for both people. It is difficult truly to understand another person's point of view, especially when he or she is not saying what you want to hear. It is also hard to be respectful of another when your own feelings have been hurt.

A relationship requires that couples communicate their changing feelings and needs. To expect perfect communication is certainly unrealistic. However, between here and perfection there is a lot of room for growth. Many couples mistakenly think that their inability to communicate in a successful and loving way means that they don't love each other enough. Certainly love has a lot to do with it, but communication skill is a much more important ingredient. More importantly, it's a learnable skill.

FORGIVENESS AND LETTING GO RESENTMENT OFTEN COMES FROM A HEART THAT HAS BEEN HURT AND BROKEN.

One of so many wonderful lessons during the lifetime of my mother was that she would teach my siblings and me that we must be good in life, do well by others and learn to forgive those who wronged us. She would often tell us that there will be times in our lives when we are going to encounter the various trials of life, and sometimes we will suffer the wrong and hurt others will have causes upon us but we must be willing to forgive.

To forgive and let go of resentment provides freedom from guilt and enables us to be in right relationship with God and our mate. When you are wronged by someone and feel terribly hurt, the pain makes it very difficult to forgive, especially when the pain is caused by your mate, whom you trust the most. The wounds from such hurt and pain can be very deep, but in this life we learn to receive blows and to forgive those who insult us. As we forgive and let go of the bitterness, anger and hurt, it is the beginning of the healing process. It brings about deliverance and release to the wounded.

When I was a little boy, I recall thinking how blessed we were due to the hard work of my mother and father, but most of all due to the prayers and faith of my mother. Because of their commitment and dedication we were able to live a good and decent life. My mother was dedicated to the church; therefore we were in church every Sunday, Sunday night, Tuesday and Friday nights. She was a woman of faith who loved the Lord. My mother brought us, (my brothers, sisters and myself) up in the Church of God in Christ, a Holiness church. My father was a deacon in another church where the rules were not so strict.

My mother was a courageous woman; she encountered many disappointments in her life but the Lord would always see her through with victory. She had the faith that somehow, some way the Lord would work things out for her. One of the things I loved about my mom was her remarkable faith to recover from trials and the adversities of life.

As life would have it, my dad started making many bad choices and committing wrong acts, including gambling and drinking. Then there was a breakdown in communication. As little kids, it gave us great joy and safety to see the closeness and communication of the union of our mom and dad. But then many nights he would come home drunk, mostly on weekends, and there would be times he would not come home until one or two days later. There were times my dad came home drunk, with no money from his paycheck for my mother to pay the bills and buy food with for the week. So how would he justify that? He would tell my mother she is giving all of his money to the church, therefore he would order her to stay home on Friday nights, which was his main night for going out before coming home after he got paid.

I recall one time there was a revival at our church and my mother wanted to go so bad, she asked my dad if he would take us and go with us so they may receive prayer that God would bless their marriage and our home. But my dad said "no!" And that she "must not go but stay home." So he went on out as always to be with the guys and gals that night. But my mother decided to go to church anyway, just as long as we get back home before my dad would as we had done a few other times in the past.

That being the last night of the revival, it was wonderful, even as a little kid I was feeling blessed as other children. By my mom forgot how late it was getting and realized it was time for us to be getting home. When we arrived home that night all was well, my dad's car was not in the driveway so we thought we had made it home before he did. My dad had come home in his drunkenness to get the food money from my mom to go back out to continue his drinking and entertaining. But after realizing we were not at home but in church, he was very upset, and the fact that he was drunk, made matters worse. I remember him teaching us not to use alcohol by telling us these words, *"when you drink alcohol you are giving you brain over to another control system, when you drink you are irresponsible from that point on."*

What we did not know was that he had hidden his car in back of the house. My mother knew something was not right, but as kids we thought it was "all-good" we had got home before dad did. As we entered the house my dad jumped from behind the door and pushed my mother to the floor and said " I told you not to go to that church tonight, and give them my money." In his moment of anger he wanted to hit her but was afraid. My mother was crying and said to him, "I am sorry for going against your will by going to church. But I just had to be there tonight, here is the food and bill money. I did not put any of it in church as you said." As little children we were very upset to see our dad conduct himself that way. But It was what my mother said afterward that was astonishing to me and I have not forgotten it to this day. She said to him **"in my hurt and pain, I forgive you for what you have done."** Now we had never seen our dad go that far before in his drunkenness and anger. As little kids we were bewildered and blindsided all at the same time but in his moment of anger he became very fearful as though he realized what he had done was wrong. He appeared to be confused and could not take the money from my mother and was afraid to go back out that night.

Even though the behavior of my father was unacceptable, we did love him very much because he was good to his children and taught us many good principles to live by, although his character was no longer a reflection of those principles he had taught us. The bad choices my dad had begun to make had a negative impact on our family life. Later on in life his bad behavior caused us to lose everything that he and my mother had worked so hard for. The bad decisions and other wrong turns my father took during that time also resulted in my parents' separation.

BLESSED ARE THE MERCIFUL: FOR THEY SHALL OBTAIN MERCY.

MATT.5: 7.

After the separation of my parents, my mother was left to care and provide for five children on her own. As I had stated she was a courageous woman, so often in her care and provision for the necessary needs of her children the demand was far more than the resources. But her courage was evidence of the reserve of the spiritual and moral strength on which she would draw on in times of crisis. She did not hold any animosity against my father nor would she speak evil against him. My mom did not take the wrong actions of my father as an opportunity to instill any hostility in (us) her children against our dad. She still loved our dad and knew that we did, as well as we should continue to love him.

In spite of the struggles and challenges my mom had to endure, she did not allow anger and resentment to build up in her heart that would surely prevent her from finding a peaceful way to forgive. Anger will not allow you to see clearly a peaceful solution to forgive and let go any resentment and hostility you may have against those who have wronged you. It is essential that we let go of the anger, hostility, and bitterness that keep us separated and unable to be in fellowship with others. We all have the desire to love and be loved, but in order to have healthy relationships, it is necessary that we make peace with ourselves and with our mate.

It was more than a year after the separation of my parents, and my dad was living with a young lady in another city. Later, we learned that my dad had taken very sick and there was no one to care for him. We also were informed that his friends had abandoned him in his time of need. But as soon as my mother received word of my father's illness, she went to that city where my father was, got him and brought him back to our home and cared for him as best she could. His health was so bad that she had to have him admitted into the hospital and she was there day and night. She cared for him up until he passed; my father died of cancer. My father is truly missed.

My mother taught us that no one could really have peace of mind in making peace with others without giving up some things; you have to give up the anger, the resentment, the need to blame, and the desire to punish those who have hurt you. Sometimes you may suffer with the pain of hurt, which could be so deep that it becomes very difficult to forgive or let go. But making peace and giving up the resentment that you are holding inside are steps in the right direction for peace of mind. This is a lesson that was imparted into our lives. The lesson of love and forgiveness, which my mother demonstrated well by the love and care she showed my father in his time of need and sickness. Emotional hurts can increase mental stress and broken relationships and can result in a violation of God's commandment to love. We are not to love the wrong behavior that a person does but we must have the love of Christ in us to forgive them that we may be forgiven.

The thought of a wrong or evil deed that a person has done to you can become difficult to forget. There are those times when we "forgiven Christians" find ourselves in a state of stubbornness in forgiving those who have caused us pain. We mull over the thought of the carelessness and thoughtlessness of their action and if we are not careful in the entertainment of our thinking we will reside in an emotional state of un-forgiveness. We are called as Christians to forgive our mates for wrong deeds they have done and not hold resentment in our heart; it is or should be part of our DNA that connects us to Christ who is our source.

THE PAIN OF ANGER

In despair, people begin to use negative tactics to force their mate to be more loving. They withhold their affection and become emotionally distant. They become irritable and critical. They attack and blame: "why don't you . . . . ?" "Why do you always . . . . ?" "How come you never . . . . .?" they fling these verbal stones in a desperate attempt to get their mate to be warm and responsive or to express whatever positive traits of affection their mate are withholding. They believe that if they give their mate enough pain, he/she will return back to their former loving ways. What makes people believe that hurting their mate will make them behave more loving? If we could just simply tell each other in plain old English that we want, more affection or attention or lovemaking or freedom or whatever it is that we are desiring at the time.

When couples don't tell each other what they want and constantly criticize each other for missing the boat, the spirit of love and cooperation disappears. In its place comes the grim determination of the power struggle, in which each one tries to force the other to meet his or her needs. Even though their mate reacts to these maneuvers with renewed hostility, they persevere. Why? Because in their unconscious minds they fear that if their needs are not met, they will die. This is a classic example of what we call the "repetition compulsion," the tendency of human beings to repeat ineffective behaviors over and over again.

Anger is destructive to a relationship, no matter what its form. When anger is expressed in a hurtful and destructive way, the person on the receiving end of the attack feels brutalized, whether or not there has been any physical violence; the old brain does not distinguish between choices of weapons. Furthermore, because of the strange workings of the subconscious, the person who unleashes the anger feels equally assaulted, because on a deeper level the old brain perceives all action as inner directed. Just as the goodwill that we extend to our mates is believed to be intended for us, the animosity that we send out is repackaged for home delivery.

When we are upset, disappointed, frustrated or angry, we find it very difficult to communicate lovingly. When negative emotions come up, we tend momentarily to lose our loving feelings of trust, caring, understanding, acceptance, appreciation and respect. At such times, even with the best intentions, talking turns into fighting. In the heat of the moment, we do not remember how to communicate in a way that works for our mate or for us.

In difficult times like these, it is said that women unknowingly tend to blame their man and make him feel guilty for his actions. Instead of realizing that he may be doing the best he can at that time. A woman could assume the worst and sound critical and resentful. When she feels a surge of negative feelings, it is especially difficult for a woman to speak in a trusting, accepting and appreciative way. And in the heat of the moment she may not realize how negative and hurtful her attitude is to her mate.

On the other hand when men are upset, they tend to become judgmental of the woman's feelings. Instead of remembering that she is vulnerable and sensitive, a man may forget her needs and sound mean and uncaring. When he feels a surge of negative feelings, it is especially difficult for him to speak in a caring, understanding, and respectful way. In the heat of the moment he may not realize how hurtful his negative attitude is to her.

When we hurt our mate, we invariably hurt ourselves. With both parties feeling under attack, there is an immediate downturn in the relationship. There is no way the two individuals can relate peaceably except if they both are willing to be considerate of each others' feelings in a loving and respectable way. There can be no intimacy because there is no safety. One might say that the old brain will not allow its defense to be penetrated.

Deep emotional wounds caused in a relationship can be a major hindrance making it extremely difficult for some to openly forgive their mate who has caused such pain. The hurt can be so overwhelming that bringing themselves to the point of forgiving may not be so easy. Unhappy people are consumed by anger and resentment. They are critical; they live in fear; they worry and they procrastinate; they wallow in self-pity and depression; they try to change their mate instead of themselves. But we must not allow our hurt and disappointment to hinder us from releasing all of our ill feelings and resentments.

Finally, we have bought into the idea that unhappy people should not have to stay in an unhappy marriage. We also have given credence to the idea that when trouble comes you should just change partners, when the truth is that the way you are living with the person must be changed. Rather than getting rid of your mate and keeping the problem, you should get rid of the problem so that you can keep your mate.

CHAPTER 9
LUST, SEX AND LIES . . .
WHY DO FOOLS FALL IN LOVE?

Studies show that people, who are so desperately in need of a relationship, often have a low concept of themselves. They often feel the reason they are not in a loving relationship is because something is wrong with them. People with low concept feel very poorly about themselves and can become oversensitive about their appearance and things that are important to them. They get to the point where they just hope that someone—anyone, practically will come into their lives, fall in love with them and they'll get married and everything will work out fine.

During the time I was waiting in my office to meet with a couple concerning some issues they were having with their personal finances, I was engaged in a conversation with one of my deacons and another young man who happen to be there at the time. We were in a discussion, which also include the subject on people who have a low concept of themselves. The young man said; "One thing I would like to say to your question pastor, is this, before I had cleaned up my sinful ways and became a member of this church, while I was still out in the world I learned in dealing with women, if you were looking for a one night stand it was always easy to get a woman in bed who had a low-concept of herself. Usually just a few words of flattery is all it takes"

He continues, "I think that women who seem to have a low concept fail to love themselves first, and they also fail to have a positive self worth of who they are. It could be that some of them have come out of a bad relationship or family abuse, I don't know but whatever it is, I do know that until they learn to love themselves first, they are only setting themselves up for further abuse. Women who are negative of their existence, self-conscious and oversensitive make poor love decisions, they feel that they have to give more just to get less; they don't feel important enough to expect anything more. My last point is this, so many of our women are shallow, they will reward you with sex just for flattering them with words to make them feel good. If they love themselves first, they will feel good and set high standards to live by."

So many of our sisters hold negative feelings of themselves concerning their looks. They are too ashamed or afraid to admit their desire for a mate; one reason is because they are unhappy with their appearance. This could be a major part in why they are still single today. They believe they are too big, too dark skinned, too ugly, their hair is too short and on and on to be attractive to get a mate. And usually this is a self-fulfilling prophecy, not because those things are necessarily true. It could be because they make no effort in the presentation of their attractiveness.

It is well understood that we also communicate with our appearance. You can present yourself in a way that says, I enjoy being who I am, and I enjoy being attractive. Whatever part of your appearance you feel makes you less attractive, it is God's creation of you, accept it and be a good steward of it. "Work with what you got". You can work to make yourself as attractive as you can, every pound of you, even if you have to work around it or over it.

Each of us could probably find a long list of reasons to dislike ourselves. On other occasions some may even hate themselves. There may be times you feel that no one had ever experienced what you are going through and you try to hide your insecurities behind false fronts, all while fooling yourself as you try to fool others.

Feelings of inferiority cause a person to evident himself or herself in daydreaming. Their daydreaming becomes an effort to escape reality. The twist in this is the more you daydream, the poorer you feel about yourself. Even though all may daydream once in a while, the person with deep feelings of inferiority will spend a great deal of time spinning fantasies. They do this to really escape the reality of how poorly he or she feels about himself or herself, believing this make-believe state of mind is supposed to be better than life.

For someone who feels inferior, these negative feelings could affect you in a number of ways. You think everyone in staring at you. You may feel extremely self-conscious when you walk in a room. You wonder what they are saying about you. Do you look OK? What do I do with myself, do

I sit or stand? Is there any place to hide? You say to yourself, only if this room could go very dark that I may exit.

A low concept of yourself can be a hindrance to forming healthy relationships. Before being in a relationship with anyone else, you need to love yourself and have positive self worth of who you are. If you don't love you, why should anyone else? So many people have unconsciously created bad relationships for themselves, simply because they have not learned to love nor accept who they are first. Hating ourselves not only hinders our response to others but can also hinder others' response to us. If you are oversensitive about your appearance or what others think of you, you become unable to focus on those things that are more important to you.

A low concept may cause you to resist authority. Whenever we don't like the way we are made, we begin to think that life has somehow cheated us. Consciously or unconsciously we develop the attitude that the world owes us something. This attitude produces bitterness against parents, school authorities, police, employers, and others.

A poor self-concept will influence your choice of a marital partner; the person who lacks self-respect often picks a mate who will devalue, criticize, or put you down. Why? To recreate the feelings to which you have become accustomed to. While others will choose a mate who is a model of virtue and achievement, if you do not feel secure and worthwhile at the very core of your self-being, you will more likely make poor choices for your mate.

A low self-concept will affect your sex life in marriage. Society has taught us that in order to win a mate we must become preoccupied with our physical appearance. It has become a consuming passion for both sexes to be more captivating to the eye. Therefore, if we feel we don't have the perfect body size, it tends to make us dissatisfied with the body we have. If you don't like your body; if you are not tall enough or your breasts are too small or your legs are too thin or your lips too big or your skin too dark, you will find it difficult to understand how anyone else could find your body appealing. The feeling of insecurity and low self-concept makes people resign themselves to negative outcomes that could potentially be reversed.

PRESSURE

Those things that should be the joy of falling in love can quickly turn into sorrow if you are falling in love for all the wrong reasons. Can there be a wrong reason for falling in love? In spite of what you may think, the answer is yes. There are many reasons why people decide to have relationships other than being in love. Getting involved with someone for the wrong reason is one of the ways in which we create unhealthy and unfulfilling relationships.

Pressure is the influence that your friends, family, society, and your own programming have place upon you that gives the message, "you should be in a relationship, and if you are not something is wrong with you." When we feel pressure by these outside influences or our own internal ones, we may choose to get involved in relationships we normally would not choose.

Whether the pressure comes from your family, your friends, or from your own sense of urgency, the results are the same: you may compromise your standards for an acceptable partner just to have a relationship with someone. It could be that when you give in to the pressure that is put on you whether by family or friends to hurry into a relationship you may be robbing yourself of the chance to experience true love and happiness. The important factor that we should consider is to develop positive feelings of self-worth.

When you make the decision to be with someone because of the pressure you feel rather than because the person seems right for you, you are giving your power away and possibly contributing to an unhappy end to your love story. Sometimes females sense that the male she is dating is loosing interest in her, and she will try to hold him by making sex more available and by actually becoming sexually aggressive. This attitude has led to many unplanned pregnancies and premature marriages.

When a man respects a woman and her values, he will generally exercise restraint. But on the other hand, when the woman gives in to pressure and feels that the only way she is going to keep a man is by having sex with him, she looses respect for herself. She is psychologically in a mind set that in order to receive love, she must give sex. Thereby loosing her self-respect, and turning away from her standards and values. When it comes to reputation however, in most cases the woman has more to lose than the man.

As I finished preaching one Sunday afternoon at one of the churches I assumed pastor-ship at. A young lady who was a member of the congregation, (let us call her Betty to protect her identity) came into my office feeling very sad and disappointed over a foolish decision she made that jeopardized her health, safety, and reputation. Betty was crying and asked me, "Do you have time to speak with me just for a moment, Pastor Johnson?" She said, "I have a problem and need to be back in fellowship with the Lord, I am pregnant and I don't know whether I have contracted HIV." So I said sure by all means please have a seat! Betty came to me hurt, fearful and crying. Why? Because she got pregnant from a one nightstand with someone she did not even know and now fearful of the unknown.

This was her first time being engaged in sexual intercourse; Betty had kept herself by standing firm on her own values and standards. Up until that day she had done well. She stated that "A few months back me and my friend-girl had gone to the mall to do some shopping. While we were there two young men came up to us and offered to buy us lunch and we accepted their offer, we then went over to the food court in the mall and ate.

After eating we got into their car and went for a ride with them whom neither one of us knew, I know that I should not have made such a foolish decision as this, but in the heat of the moment I did and caused hurt upon myself. We were taken to a city park so they could have sex with us. I was not going to do anything, I was just going to let my friend do it but they kept on pressuring me so I did it to. He said he promise he was not going to get me pregnant. We processed to have sex and he had "accidentally" gone all the way and did not stop until it was too late. I was "under pressure to have sex with him" my friend and the guy she was with was doing it. So they pressured me to do it with him. I did not mean to do it, it was an accident."

She also stated how hurt and embarrassed she was when she met him about four months later, he was with another young lady, she said; "He acted like he did not know who I was. He showed no respect for me nor did he say anything nice for the baby I was carrying for him, he said to me; "What you are carrying is yours, don't step to me with that, get rid of it or go tell some other guy you was messing around with." This young man has also moved to another state with his girlfriend. Betty is now left to care and provide for this child all on her own as so many of our young girls is. Betty is also being tested for the next six months to see if she has contracted a sexually transmitted disease.

If we really look at this situation it was not an "accident." She should have said that her emotions got out of control and they went all the way. The inevitable happened, sex!! *(You always have the power and the right to say No!)* She willfully made a series of decisions that permitted it to happen. She willingly agreed with him and the other party to seek out a place for this to happen. She also participated in the kissing and hugging and in the heat of the moment she agreed to have intercourse with this looser. She agreed when she permitted it to happen with a looser that she did not even know his name. Our hope now for Betty is that she did not contract a sexually transmitted disease along with being pregnant.

To call this progression of activities an "accident" is a self-deceiving rationalization. The fact is that she refused to draw the line as so many of our girls do. There were several stopping points along the way where she had the opportunity to say no! This was with someone whom she did not know which gives greater reason to say no. She threw her self-respect, moral standards and spiritual values out the window. This is not an accident but a choice, a choice to have premarital sex, which leads so many of our young girls to unwanted pregnancy and sexually transmitted disease. With AIDS being the 3rd. leading cause of death among African-American women from age 25 to 34, African-American women lead the nation in unplanned pregnancy.

AFRICAN-AMERICAN WOMEN ARE AT A HIGHER RISK OF PREGNANCY-RELATED DEATH.

African-American women are dying from pregnancy-related complications three times more frequently than any other racial group, according to New Centers for Disease Control and Prevention data. Death within one year of pregnancy typically occurs from complication such as blood clots, hemorrhage and heart problems.

African-American women must take better care of themselves, your heath is more important than your hair. It's important that you get a proper risk assessment from your doctor. Because getting early prenatal care that will include ultrasounds, which can diagnose any potentially fatal illnesses is very important. You should set up an appointment to see a doctor well before you get pregnant.

"Pregnancy is a joyful time, but not without its risks," says Dr. Renee Volny, obstetrician-gynecologist and a health policy follow at The Satcher Health Leadership Institute in Atlanta. "Pregnancy puts physical stress on some of the body's vital organs."

Early prenatal care is the most important way a woman can prevent her risk of pregnancy-related death. African-American mothers are almost three times more likely than white mothers to wait until the third-trimester to seek prenatal care, or not at all. Of those who have no prenatal care, the risk of death is five times greater.

"Without the proper risk assessment by a doctor, a woman may not realize that a pregnancy could put her life at risk," said Dr. Valny, "This is why women should try to see a doctor well before they actually get pregnant."
In fact, the study authors explain that some of the women's pre-pregnancy health conditions were just as important risk factors in pregnancy-related death.

Once pregnant, early prenatal care can diagnose potentially fatal illnesses. One in particular, ectopic pregnancy, where the fetus implants outside of the uterus, usually in the fallopian tube-can quickly lead to major hemorrhage and death. African-American women are actually more likely to die from ectopic pregnancy than other pregnant women. However, with early prenatal care, including ultrasound, the condition can be diagnosed and treated before it becomes fatal.

LONELINESS AND DESPERATION

We all may have experienced loneliness at one time or another. It is a period in your life when you felt so emotionally empty that you may have found yourself desperate for someone to love and to be loved by. But unfortunately, what may start out as a lonely act of reaching out to another human being can end in a very complicated and hurtful relationship out of desperation. When you are feeling lonely or desperate, you are much more likely to make poor love choices and end up in unfulfilling relationships. If you allow your emotional vulnerability to influence your choice of finding your partner, you could be ensuring yourself to end up in an unhappy relationship

If you are not emotionally sound due to the loneliness or desperation, you will make poor choices in the partners whom you bring into your life. The feeling of urgency will have you to choose someone you know is not right for you. The desperation will cause you to choose to be involved in a relationship that you know is doomed from the start and is sure to create unfortunate circumstances in your life. To get involved with people for the wrong reason is a sure way of creating complications and robbing yourself of happiness.

First of all, you must learn to appreciate self and see the valuable person you are, love and accept yourself and be unwilling to lower your standards just because you are feeling emotionally vulnerable due to your loneliness. Although you could be experiencing some urgency and the need to belong, it may be a tough moment in your life but time will heal, so allow it to happen. As a young man, I would often hear my mother say to my sisters, "You are not a store trying to get rid of some old merchandise that is put on sale." You are a valuable kind of lovable human being who deserves to have the kind of relationship you want, not just the kind you think you have to settle for. Neither should you be so needy by trying to make things happen for you in way of a relationship. And then justify your decision by convincing yourself that this is all you can get because you are too desperate to wait and carefully pick someone who is right for you. What we should understand is that when you are comforted with who you are and walking in integrity you don't have to accept the negative labels people are trying to put on you. You do not have to be rushed into a relationship by negative talk. To pick someone as a life partner and soul mate is a decision that should not be made lightly.

Ellen was lonely and desperate. Her biological clock was ticking although she has two children already by two different men, her hope and dreams were that some day she would have a complete family of her own, husband and kids. After much searching on the Internet, joining dating sites and church socials, she finally found someone who swept her off her feet and "He is a successful brother." She met him through an online dating service. For a very short while they communicated online and he presented himself well to her. But little does Ellen know her newfound love, Jerald, and his friend Toni were living a dubious secret life. The names of the three persons have been changed to protect their identity.

Soon afterward a family member informed Ellen of her man's strange characteristics and unusual activities. Ellen became very angry with this family member for telling such a (as she calls it) lie. "No not my man!! Not Jerald!! I know him he loves me. How could you come here and tell all those false allegations against Jerald? You are just jealous because Jerald is not yours, and you don't have a man, and don't want you talk to me anymore." After many months had passed all seemed well. Ellen and the kids were happy and Jerald had asked Ellen to marry him. Ellen was very excited because she was also five months pregnant and was going to have his baby.

Ellen was now in her last month of pregnancy. After returning home from her appointment with the doctor. Ellen entered her house and heard an unusual sound coming from her bedroom. She proceeded straight down the hall to the bedroom because no one should have been home during this time of the day. What a shock!! Much to Ellen surprise, she discovered that her soon to be husband Jerald and his friend Toni were in bed together engaged in a homosexual affair. Her man Jerald and Toni had been living a secret lie; they have been involved in sexual activities with one another for more than five years. As you can guess this discovery was an extreme emotional shock to her, her man with another man together, engaged in sex.

"It all seemed so unreal to me, it was like I was a dead person. I could not bring myself to believe that I actually was alive and standing in that room to see these two men having sex. This foolishness was inconceivable for me to visualize in my mind that this was really happening before me, I could have believed any other bad report about him than this, because he said he loved only me. How could he lie to me like that? What could I have done to deserve this? This man, or whatever he is, has ruined our lives, but all is not lost, my children and I will make it." Jerald and his lover Toni were put away from Ellen's home with an understanding from her two "big brothers" never to return. Ellen said Jerald's only explanation for such deception, "You were desperate, weak and vulnerable, you made yourself available to be deceived."

Ellen was unable to bring her unborn baby to full birth; she stated that this was due to the physiological damage and emotional trauma to her mind and body. She stated; "Now as I look back on this experience there were many warning signals. But I was a fool in love, too blind to see. I was not going to ruin my relationship with my man on some unfounded suspicion. I had convinced myself that these warning signals are only insufficient evidence; there is no proof that anything is going on between Jerald and Toni, they are just close friends. But now that this is all over with, I owe a number of people an apology and also my children and I must make good on this right a way. As wrong and deceiving as Jerald was, I also must take some responsibility for these unfortunate circumstances. I allowed my emotions to take the place of me making sound decisions; it frightens me to think that I allowed that man to be over my children. Yes, I was a fool in love and refused to open my eyes, to see what kind of man I had in my house over my children."

If there could be any straight forward take or lesson learned from the perils of Ellen's experience, it would be that, parents should pay very close attention to their lovers around their children. Be sure that you are not putting your children at risk or exposing them or yourself to any harm. And if you are seeking for your mate online, keep in mind that anyone can present him or herself well on paper or on your computer monitor, but the character of that person may not be who you were made to believe they were. You could not only meet someone that is not right for you, but someone who is life threatening to you and your loved ones.

You are only being a wise and responsible parent to take a good look into your potential mate's background. What you have in your care now is too precious to lose.

For the most part, falling in love has to be the highest human experience one can have. Therefore to fall in love into a knowingly unhealthy relationship is somewhat repeating your past mistakes. There is this quote by George Santayana: "Those who cannot remember the past are condemned to repeat it." None of us can completely escape from the influences of our past. But by remembering our past and maybe if there were mistakes made along the way we give ourselves time to heal and adjust these wrongs within us. We can turn the pain of our poor choices into some wonderful teachable moments that can help us in creating the healthy and loving relationships we desire.

Personally I think that one of the most wonderful feelings anyone can have in a relationship, is having someone in your life that you feel safe with. In every healthy relationship there is some chemistry of healing in it, therefore to be with someone who is a loving, caring, and understanding person who has good character, you both can work together to heal the wounds of hurt and pain in each of you. Out of all the things that are happening in our lives each day some may not be contributing to your happiness. You should look for positive things that make you happy, watch the company you keep.

SEXUAL HUNGER

" There she was looking so sexy with that very-short dress on revealing everything about herself from her breasts down to her fine legs. Her physical attraction was very stimulating to my hormones. This lady had the most incredible smile showing off her beautiful white teeth. She seems to have no shame in her game, allowing me to see all that she was revealing for public view. Now I thought that I was stronger than this but the <u>temptation was overwhelming</u>, this fine thing did not even have on any underwear, none at all.

The excitement of my hormones was mounting, her body was banging! And all I knew was that <u>I had to</u> <u>have her at any cost.</u> I was visualizing what she and I could be doing if I could get with that fine thing. She was enjoying the attention she was getting from me so I decided to go over to inquire her name. She told me and I gave her my name. I thought at this point to use one of my more common approach lines that we men use on women when we really want to get with them. I use the flattery approach on her, *"you have such a banging body girl <u>I can not hardly</u> <u>control myself!</u> And your eyes are so beautiful!"* "When using such lines as this we know that it reinforces what they want to hear whether her physical appearance is attractive or not, they are flattered."

He continues; "As I was touching and feeling any part of her body I wanted to, she seem to have no shame or reservations of my sexual motives. So I asked her for a date and she said" "OK! How about later tonight?" "I tried not to appear to be surprised at her reply that she would agree so quickly to my advances. I asked her can I pick her up by 8p.m. this evening? She said" "You tell me where to meet you and I will be there." "At that point I thought there may be a problem of some kind, so I asked, "Why can I not pick you up?" I was embarrassed to even ask her why, after she had allowed me to carry on as I did but I asked anyway, "Are you married?" Not expecting her to say that she really was married, not at all, not by the way she was dressed and how she was conducting herself and allowing me to do what I was doing to her.

Her reply to my question was, "yes, I am married but don't worry it's OK I am loosing interest in him anyway and I need to relieve myself of all this sexual tension. You tell me where to meet you and I will be there, I promise!" "So pastor Johnson, we agreed on a time and place for that evening, and after she arrived we had a few drinks, then we went to a motel to have sex but in the midst of drinking and building up to that moment I forgot that <u>I did not have a condom</u>. But I said to myself <u>what is the concern? She seems to be very clean</u> <u>and does not appear to be like anyone who would have a disease</u>. As she was undressing herself and kissing on the sensitive parts of my body I began to loose interest in a condom, she reassured me in my decision by saying," "<u>there is nothing to worry about baby,</u> you and my husband are the only ones." "Now with me being under pressure of sexual tension I gave up on the idea of a condom. I desperately wanted to be with this girl, the excitement and arousing situation mounting was so intense, it gave me a strong need to relieve myself in her.

The sexual experience she and I engaged in was wonderful (<u>although I had this</u> <u>dangerous feeling in the back of my mind that something is not right</u>) she did everything I wanted her to do to my body and gave me the kind of pleasure I was not expecting her to do being that she was a married woman. After we ended our sexual intercourse I was expecting her to feel some remorse for what had just happened, as I was feeling being that this lady was married. But she was not remorseful at all, in fact she felt good about every things that had just happen, and agreed to continue to meet with me and give me sexual pleasure. I was surprised this married woman wanted to continue to have sex with me but she did. She and I continued to meet and engaged in intercourse. There were times that it really seemed like <u>she had just had</u> <u>sex with someone else but I concluded on</u> <u>the thought by saying, there is nothing to be concerned</u> <u>about, so we did it</u>. I later learned that she did not have time for me anymore because <u>there were other sexual partners</u> <u>she was involved with.</u> I was hurt but later I learned the real reason why she did not want to see me anymore.

Today pastor Johnson, two years later as I sit here in this hospital, I am waiting to receive treatment and get my medication for this sexually transmitted disease HIV, I wish I had paid attention to all of the warning signs and used better judgment. Now I don't know what is going to happen. I am just taking one day at a time. If I could have controlled myself, things would have been different for me. I could have been married to a nice clean young lady whom at the time I thought had her standards too high and she wanted to wait until she was married. Now I wish I could have paid more attention to her, she was right. She once told me;" "You don't really know what you are getting yourself into when you are involved in a relationship with someone who is actively engaged in sexual intercourse with many partners." "Yes, pastor Johnson, she was right!"

Before you read any further, please go back to the top of sexual hunger and read over a second time the words that are under-lined. Thank you.

To protect the identity of these two young people we will call them bro Bob and Annie Bee. Brother Bob became a member of my church about eight months before he passed. He was diagnosed with full-blown AIDS and other related medical conditions. The last report I received of Ms. Annie Bee is that she is still alive with the disease and sexually active with other men, married and unmarried. With sexual hunger you may not even feel attracted to the person you get involved with. You just want to be with someone and have sex.

To those reading the dramatic consequences of Brother Bob testimony in my book, if you are still going to continue to be engaging in premarital sex, please!! Take advantage of the uses of condoms, contraceptives and other protection that is available. And if you proceed with premarital sex in spite of the facts that are out there concerning sexually transmitted diseases, proceed in the best way possible for both of you and for everyone else concerned. In other words, if you are going to engage in sex before marriage anyway please, use protection!! Condoms are effective in protection against HIV/AIDS. Allow this to be a deciding moment for the both of you. "And, get tested together."

To avoid a profound disappointment in your life and especially to our young people, I must say again be informed. Information and knowledge are powerful tools in the fight against HIV. Get tested, and those of you who are actively engaged in premarital sex, for your personal health you should get treated. Knowing your status is greater than doubt, knowing your HIV status can save yours and others lives. As a people we must learn to speak openly, discuss HIV/AIDS with your partner, children, friends and family.

To ignore or overlook these conversations by not engaging in dialogue will reinforce the stigma that allows the disease to spread in our communities as it is today. The figures are dismal. And as most medical personnel will tell you, Blacks are disproportionately impacted on all measures when it comes to HIV/AIDS.

The truth is in the numbers, just to speak of a few; 38% of Blacks at age 13 to 29 account for the nearly 25,000 infections estimated to occur on an annual basis. 20% of Black youth progressed to AIDS within one year of receiving an initial HIV diagnosis because they are often diagnosed late in the course of infection. 45% of Blacks account for nearly half of new HIV infections each year. AIDS is the 3RD leading cause of death among Black women ages 25 to 34 and Black men ages 35 to 44. And lastly: 44% of Black Americans name media as their primary source of information about HIV/AIDS, far more than any other single source, including family or health care providers, according to a Kaiser Family Foundation national survey.

And remember, there is nothing so bad in your life that you are ashamed of that you can't come to the Lord about, He knows anyway. The Lord cares for you and He wants to set you free from all your troubles, guilt, and stain. But you must open up to Him, surrender to Him and He will make you whole.

Once you can admit the personal guilt, you can move on to the second step, which is to confess your wrong and ask God to forgive you. In the Holy Bible it reads; "If we confess our sins, He is faithful and just and will forgive us of our sins and purify us from all unrighteousness. 1 John

1:9. (lab.) He is our heavenly Father who will totally and completely forgive our sins when we repent. If we face up to our wrong and are sincerely sorry, God has a wonderful way of using these experiences for our good. He can help us through our experiences to become stronger, wiser, and a more complete person. When others are entrapped and enslaved in sin, your attitude toward your experiences can help you to grow to be more loving, understanding, and sympathetic to them.

CHAPTER 10

BETRAYAL; YOU SAID THAT YOU LOVE ME, AND ONLY ME, SO WHY ARE YOU IN BED WITH..?

My intent is not to be judgmental or preach to you, the same as in my writing of this chapter as with other chapters in this book. I seek only to bring some measure of understanding to these matters. My only hope is that we can derive at a new level of understanding in relationships.

"You have heard that it was said, `Do not commit adultery. But I tell you that anyone who looks at a woman lustfully has already committed adultery with her in his heart." Matt. 5: 27,28. (niv.) In the Old Testament under the law it is said that it was wrong for any person to have sex with someone other than his or her spouse (Exodus 20:14). But Jesus makes it very clear to us that the desire to have sex with someone other than your spouse is mental adultery and therefore it is sin. Jesus emphasized that if the act of committing adultery is wrong then the desire and willingness to commit that act is wrong.

To be faithful to your spouse with your body but not your mind is to break the trust that is so vital to a strong marriage. Jesus is not condemning any of us for having natural interest in the opposite sex nor is He condemning us for our healthy sexual desire. But He does condemn the deliberate and repeated filling of one's mind with fantasies that would or could be acted upon. Lust can be understood as a mentally broken relationship with your spouse.

Broken relationships whether they are physical or mental that are due to sexual involvement hinders our relationship with God. We are hypocrites when we claim to love God but we are not faithful mentally or physically to our spouse. When we practice self-control, it is good but Christ wants us each day to also practice "thought—control" as well. Our attitude toward our spouse and the commitment of that relationship in so many ways reflects our relationship with God.

Lust is a dangerous emotion that is always threatening to leap out of control, which leads to the committed act. These un-controlled emotions violate our commitment to our spouse and our stand with Christ, thereby causing us to be held accountable for our wrong and uncontrolled attitude. If you have a problem controlling your flesh it is a serious problem that needs to be resolved as soon as possible, don't wait!! It is a sinful problem that needs to be resolved now. Your faithfulness and commitment to your spouse depends on you to do the right thing. Sinful lust is an evil emotion that violates God's commandment and will for us to faithfully love our spouse.

You may have the question in your mind to ask, if lustful thoughts are sin, why not go ahead and do the lustful actions too what's the difference? Well, allow me to answer your question saying this; anyone who is acting out sinful lustful desires the committed act is harmful to them in many ways. Acting out sinful desires causes people to excuse sin and seek reasons to justify it rather than to stop sinning altogether. Acting out these sinful emotions destroys trust and the marriage itself as well as a deliberate direct rebellion against God's word. This sinful, selfish action always hurts someone else in addition to the sinner. When you really think about it un-controlled sinful action is more dangerous than sinful desires. There are physical and emotional reasons why sinful desires should not be acted out. Not withstanding, sinful desires are just as damaging to your righteousness as any un-Godly sinful acts are. When this lustful emotion is left unchecked, wrong desires will result in wrong actions and these wrong actions destroys relationships as well as families and turns people away from God.

When we at anytime tolerate the sin of lust in our lives and allow it to go unchecked it could eventually destroy us as well as our marriage. It is always better to get rid of the wrong things we treasure, bad and sinful habits even though the removal of it may be painful, than to allow the sin of that thing to bring judgment and condemnation upon you. You should often examine your life for anything that could cause you to sin and break the relationship with your spouse. You should carefully and surely take every necessary step to get rid of the wrong sinful desires and actions that hinders your relationship with Christ, and your mate.

VOWS

Marriage vows are "sacred." Even if the vows which the couple make are made outside any religious connotation, to which the word "sacred" is most often tied in our understanding, the very fact of making vows to one other, of making and keeping promises, recognizes that there is something that transcends the two, male and female individually. That which transcends for some may be the relationship itself, or for those who believe, they will tell you it is that which goes beyond the relationship, God Himself the creator of all things. Some will speak of it in other terms, perhaps in a quite amorphous fashion. There is, nonetheless, a sense of the transcendent in their coming together, a feeling of something beyond themselves, which is at the center of their tie to each other.

Now the marriage ceremony sanctions the vows in the double sense of making them lawful and bringing them under law. The will of the individual is transformed by church and state into a moral and legal responsibility with the primary intent of insuring the permanence of the relationship. Whatever their personal motives may be, individuals who choose to marry are asking the civil and religious community to acknowledge and enforce their promises, their future responsibility to abide by their present intent. In this act, they surrender some of their right of self-determination. The couples who desire to make their bond a permanent one receive the assistance of others in making their desires and intention "lawful" that is, the structure within which they agree to shape future decisions and actions.

Marriage is the highest form of interpersonal commitment and friendship achievable between two sexually attracted people. When sacred vows are declared between the couple it is understood that these vows are to be a "total commitment" that is required. It is an unreserved dedication of one's whole self to the relationship. One's faith perspectives become important here, because there will certainly be a connection between one's world view, or life values, and one's willingness or ability to dedicate the self, without reservation, to anything!

The second point is "accepting commitment," something which is repeated in many ways in our relationships. This involves learning to love and value the other for the imperfect person he or she is.

This third point is crucial and is basic to the whole understanding of commitment: accepting commitment is an act of "grace." Love is a gift, is given freely, and must be received as that, a gift. We cannot earn or deserve the other's love when it is given in an act of grace.

THE BETRAYAL

When the storms of unfaithfulness and betrayal break through the sacred vows of your marriage you go from happiness to extreme sorrow, from peace to perplexity. Within a matter of moments your world is turned upside down. The pain of hurt, shame and embarrassment takes you for what seems like a never-ending ride on the roller coaster of sorrow and hailstorm. You thought this marriage would last forever and there was no reason that you should have expected anything less.

He would say all of the right words; do all the right things that would ensure a good and happy marriage, which caused you to build your confidence in him. He always had great respect for you and he was a man of integrity. The vows are still fresh in your mind but now seems like a nightmare; he promised to continue to love you, to comfort, honor and keep you through sickness and in health, and forsaking all others. But when "lust had conceded"(kjv.) the words in his marital vows were all meaningless to him.

THE INVISIBLE SIDE OF BETRAYAL

When we fall in love, we change, and the world changes. We're suddenly filled with energy and optimism; we are entranced, enthralled, uplifted. Once separated and defensive, we feel truly connected and involved in the world. Life's energy vibrates at a higher frequency. All the world seems to be a better place these days.

All lovers believe they have been blessed to find someone so special. "No one else has ever felt what I feel," they think, "no one has ever experienced love like this." What the lovers are expressing is "I have found that special someone who rocks my world, the one and only, whom I've been seeking, at last my love has finally come. You are everything that was missing in my life. You are going to meet all my needs. I feel like myself again, and I am no longer lonely. You will never abandon me. You have saved me."

So often he/she will say to their newfound love with all joy and admiration; "There is nothing that shall ever separate us." You promise to love me and me only; no one shall ever come between you and I, my heart my soul trusts you.

Lust is best noted as sexual craving, when it goes un-checked it becomes excessive and unrestrained. Lust will emotionally destroy the best of us mentally, and it will destroy many of us both, mentally and physically. Lust eats away at your morals and values that you once held to with integrity, lustful desires and the acting out of it are not Godly right of any morally good results.

The Bible tells us this; "but every man is tempted, when he is drawn away of his own lust, and enticed. Then when lust hath conceived, it bringeth forth sin: and sin, when it is finished, bringeth forth death. Do not err (be not deceived), my beloved brethren." James 1:14-16 (kjv).

While trying to start the counseling session, I was finally able to comfort her (to protect the identity let's call this couple Peggy and Ted) through words of encouragement and prayer; after she stopped crying and was in a stable state of mind. She said, "Pastor Johnson I am so hurt, it seems like the world and all it's evil has fallen on me. I did not see it coming. I trusted this man with my whole heart and just to think of all the things we've been through together. There was no way I thought he could ever betray my trust and confidence in him. Until he committed his wrongful act, Ted has always been an inspiration to our children and me and as you know pastor Johnson, he is the reason I am in church today. Before I met Ted, I really did not know the Lord but now He has made a difference in my life and I am thankful. What made me feel good as a wife is to have a husband as Ted who had always lived a saved life before the children and me and I love him so much. Ted was a very special person in my life, he always seems to know how to make me happy and smile, no matter how down I might be.

I never knew I was capable of feeling this way about another person again. I have been hurt in the past but I knew that relationship was no good from the start."

This young lady's husband made a foolish decision by allowing someone to coerce him into doing a wrongful deed that resulted in committing adultery, an act of stupidity which was a heavy blow to us all. It was not expected of him. His family and in-laws, his church and community all love him and he had always been a man of integrity. His conduct and behavior has always been outstanding and admired by all. Ted allowed that seed of lust to manifest in him, which caused him to make a severe offense to his sense of integrity and decency.

He came before the church with his wife and kids and asked the church and his wife to forgive him, of his wrong. He also said; " I feel foolish telling you all this I can't believe this is me. I have put myself in this situation, I blame no one but myself I put myself in this foolish situation. So, I am asking the church to please forgive me I promise that I will never betray your trust in me again."

Ted was given a second chance to redeem himself, and his wife who loves him very dearly forgave him with open arms and the church restored him back into fellowship. How often have we made a big mess of things or done something so foolish that we desperately wished for another opportunity to make it right? We all have; usually, it's as simple as a pickup line that fell flat or a meeting for which you were late because you didn't set your alarm early enough. But other times we wish for an opportunity to fix a situation that could deeply affect our lives; a job interview that didn't go well or a relationship ruined because of an unkind word or a thoughtless act. Either way, the sinking feeling that there is no way to make it better usually follows the awful realization that you messed up badly.

Many couples assume that love means never having to say you're angry, sorry, irritated, turned off, hurt or upset. The illusion of the "perfect couple" is that problems won't arise, arguments are quickly forgiven and forgotten, and differences are for other people in less "perfect" relationships. As I have said, this is the illusion of the "perfect couple."

"At first it was a dream come true." When they first met, let's just call them (Edward and Dianna,) "fell in love at first sight." Six months later after they had married, their feelings for each other were so strong that it was very difficult for them to be apart very long. But after a days work, they were finally together this couple described having sex with each other as "the best they could have imagined."

Often they would get home about the same time and they would make love on the floor in the living room, "because we could not wait until we got to the bedroom." Sometimes on long weekend drives in the country, they would pull off to the side of the road and make love "in the car, on a blanket in his father's field or other places."

Edward stated: "when Dianna and I first met it was like a dream come true for the both of us. Not just the way we made love, which was incredible, but how close we felt to each other. I believed she could read my mind, she knew exactly what I wanted and she always said the right thing. I'd never been so in love."

I asked Dianna to describe her feeling after she and Edward met, she stated: "my excitement at finding someone like Edward was a feeling that I never have had before. I felt relieved that I'd finally found a man who was honest and relaxed about our sexuality. He was not pushy or demanding like most men. He knew how to be warm, affectionate, sincere and tender. In those early days of our marriage, we used to stay up all night talking about our dreams and plans for the future. I felt like I was seventeen all over again. It was wonderful. Now here we are and all I can think about is getting out of this marriage."

I then asked Dianna to let Edward know how she felt when she discovered he was committing a sexual act with another woman. She said: " It haunted me badly to think that he would view me as being less, that he would have a desire to be with someone else to satisfy his sexual desires. I felt used and taken for granted by Edward. I felt as if I was his sexual toy for his total pleasure, without him having a true commitment to me. And before he says anything I know what I did was wrong but I only did it to get back at him for how he hurt me, he just doesn't know how that made me feel."

She then stated: "I was so mad at Edward that I wanted nothing else to do with him, I began to put up my defenses sexually and that made him mad. He would get demanding and start blaming me for being with his co-worker. I began to withdraw sexually more and more from Edward, I knew he felt rejected because he would get very angry and go into a rage. The more he demanded me to have sex with him, the more I said no! The more resentful he became the more he would try to hurt me by saying that I am whore for having sex with his co-worker.

It was just that one time that I ever messed up, and Edward knows that. I did not know any other way to make him feel how he haunted me without killing myself. And as I have said it was only to get back at Edward and he knows I would have never hurt him like that. Edward knows how much I love him, I would have never cheated on him. Edward betrayed my trust in him when he cheated on me with his ex-wife. Pastor Johnson I just wanted to die. I just could not trust him anymore after he committed that act; I didn't believe a word he said at that point. Even though he kept insisting he still loved me and asked me to forgive him, I could only think of getting out of this marriage, how could he have done such a thing? I felt like I wanted to kill him and hated the fact that I still loved him"

Afterward I asked Edward to please share some understanding on how he could allow himself to commit such inappropriate behavior to damage their marriage as he has. And to tell Dianna how her inappropriate behavior made him feel when he discovered she had cheated on him as a result of his conduct, Edward said; "Pastor Johnson, I must say first of all even though we are not a member of your church I am so pleased by your kindness to agree to meet and counsel with us. You did not have to do it and we appreciate you very much. I just needed to say that.
There is no justification for what I have done. I am truly sorry for my wrongful actions. Infidelity is what caused the split-up of my mom and dad, and I thought it was something that I would never let happen in our relationship. I should have conducted myself better than that. We have always had

a good marriage up until I deceived my wife. I came out of a bad marriage so I know how Dianna feels, because this is the kind of conduct my ex-wife was doing in our marriage with the mailman, bus driver, and my best friend who she now lives with. Pastor Johnson, it hurt me to my bones to find out that my ex-wife would do me that way, and then to discover through the court that none of the four children from our marriage were mine. Pastor Johnson, I don't know why I would have ever wanted to be with that woman again. I do know why, I allowed my "lustful spirit" to take over in me and bring me to this low not only to be with my ex-wife but women in general. I know I have a good wife, up until we allowed all this foolishness to come between us.

My problem started when I could not stop watching all of that pornography on the Internet. It seemed like the more I would watch porno the greater the lust and desire in me for more, which resulted in me having such strong lascivious feelings until I had to act out those lustful desires. I am truly sorry for what I have done. I was wrong and as I have said there is no justification for my behavior. I made the vow to to love, honor and cherish her forsaken all others, but I allowed lustful desires to overtake me. And it was foolish of me Pastor, because my wife satisfies all of my needs in every way and more.

I love Dianna but she is wrong for what she did, with my co-worker?? How does she think that makes me look? This is ridiculous, she did not have to do that; two wrongs don't make a right. Yes, that hurt me because I have to face this guy at work five days a week; it made me so mad until I wanted to end our marriage. Because of our stupidity, we both have jeopardized our health, putting ourselves at risk of HIV/AIDS. But I don't really want to lose Dianna, she wants to stay with me, and I want to stay with her. We just can't get pass this mess we both have created in our marriage through lust. So this is why we are here today before you pastor Johnson, we want to know can you work with us to help restore our marriage?"

It is obvious this couple still loves each other. After hearing the two of them admitting their wrong and unfaithfulness in their marriage, and they both are seeking help to work through the mess they had made, I was truly impressed. I said to them; "you both realize that you are still in love with each other and you want to stay together that's good, it gives us a foundation to work from. The question is whether you are motivated enough to break through this evil spirit of lust and infidelity or go your separate ways." Thankfully this couple came in early enough and both of them were still optimistic that they could save their marriage and be the beautiful loving couple they once were. To help them to regain the trust and the romance they had enjoyed in the past, I offered them some exercises and aids, which could be used with most couples. These exercises help break down the emotional blocks, sexual barriers and the unwillingness to trust.

After much counsel and work activities with Edward and his lovely wife Dianna, they were able to work through a number of their past resentments and hurt feelings by speaking their points of view briefly, in specific terms and with a commitment toward a positive outcome. Instead of blaming or accusing each other with self-righteous anger, they are now able to make eye contact; this is something they had not been able to do for a while. They now speak in a warm and loving manner, no threatening tone of voice, and their focus is on what could be done to satisfy both of their needs in the relationship. For the first time, in months they both felt that their hurt and pain were being acknowledged and understood.

I also suggested some proven points to Edward and Dianna that could help them to overcome their sexual conflicts and put more enjoyment and satisfaction into their relationship. These points have helped many couples to find that level of passion and romance that they had in their initial infatuation but a far richer sexual thrill than before.

I made Edward and Dianna well aware that their past unfaithfulness and resentment may come up from time to time. But the good that I have seen in them and their willingness to stay together, leads me to believe they are mentally and emotionally prepared to deal with them without blaming or attacking each other. Within a year this couple came back to me for counseling and just to let me know that they are still doing all of the exercises I had given them, and that they are more committed to their marriage than before. They have reached a deeper level of commitment to their marriage. These young people are now in the church and have renewed the wedding vows and they have continued to grow as individuals and as a couple.

There are so many people today who have walked away from the opportunity of redeeming themselves. To be restored or given a second chance that somehow you messed that up, our pride and insecurity makes us resign ourselves to negative outcomes that could potentially become a problem in our relationship. Because we don't think that we deserve a second chance or we can't deal with the potential embarrassment of the do-over, we often don't even try.

Why not fix the problem? Until we recognize the agenda of our vows and marriage, and cooperate with that agenda in the conduct of our relationships, our social problems of betrayal will continue to grow out of hand, and our individual lives will suffer. If we could get this situation under control, our marriage would survive and prosper.

We find these words in the book of Romans 6:15-20. It reads as follows: "For that which I do I allow not: for what I would, that do I not; but what I heat, that do I. If then I do that which I would not, I consent unto the law that it is good. Now then it is no more I that do it, but sin that dwelleth in me. For I know that in me dwelleth no good thing: for two will is present with me; but how to perform that which is good I find not. For the good that I would I do not: but the evil, which I would not, that I do. Not if I do that I would not, it is no more I that do it, but sin that dwelleth in me."(kjv).

In reading these words of the apostle Paul, we find it to be more than just the cry of one desperate man. But it also describes the experience of anyone who claims to be a Christian who feels that struggling against sin or trying to please God by keeping His word only without the help of the Holy Spirit of God living inside of you. If we intend to please God and have a good and healthy relationship with our mate, we can never underestimate the power of sin. The mistake so many people make is when they attempt to fight sin on their own strength. Satan is a crafty tempter, and we have an amazing ability to make excuses when we give in to his temptations. Instead of trying to overcome sin with human will power, we must take hold of the tremendous power of Christ that is available to us all. This is God's provision for victory over temptation and sin. If we seek Him, the Lord will send His Holy Spirit to live in us and give us power. And if we happen to fall, He will lovingly reach out to help us up.

Lust is a very strong spirit from Satan. Lust has no conscience, it doesn't care about your marriage, lust doesn't care about your responsibility, lust doesn't care if you are a preacher, teacher or the mailman, lust wants what it wants when it wants it.

Lust begins in the mind and happens out of our natural selfish desires. Lust occurs when we begin to make someone or something so important that is becomes a god unto itself. Lust is perverted love. While love is honoring and giving, lust is for taking and getting at the expense of others.

CHAPTER 11

ABUSE; FROM WARM AND LOVING TO, BATTERING RELATIONSHIPS.

It is said that men who batter represent a wide spectrum of age, race, religion, socioeconomic status, education, and careers. However, some characteristics are represented across the board. For the most part, the reports are that the abusers are men who don't feel very good about themselves, they believe that they are not worthwhile, and look to others for reassurance. He holds traditional views about sex roles and look to his partner for nearly all of his emotional support and nurturance. If he doesn't feel good about himself, he's likely to suspect that others may feel the same. So he anticipates rejection and he can perceive almost anything as a rejection.

Just to be fair in my discussion, although traditionally men are more often than not reported as the abusers to their partners in the relationship, we are now realizing more and more reports show women being the abusers. Men who are abused by their mates represent a larger part of our society than some may realize. This is what men encounter everyday by their wife/girlfriends.

Some may ask, "Does this really happen?" When a woman asks her man, "Who was that you were talking to on the phone?" or as he returns home from work and says "Baby I am home, and she says "Where in the____ have you been? You are late, you should have been home fifteen minutes a go." You duck as a plate or a glass goes flying past your head and it crashes into the wall behind you. This is not the woman being abused by her husband or boyfriend; it is the woman who is the abuser.

There are all forms and levels of physical and emotional abuse, and although men will not talk about their mates abusing them, you can be assured that this kind of abuse also happens everyday. Equally as many men, if not more, are assaulted or emotionally abused by their wife or girlfriend as women are assaulted or emotionally abused by their husband or boyfriend.

Since the abuser finds it difficult to express feelings of hurt and disappointment, he is more likely to respond with anger. Responding to perceived insults with violence increases his negative feelings about himself and makes the cycle all the more likely to recur. His limited ability to empathize makes it difficult for him to understand his mate's feelings. He has little or no insight into her pain and fear, so his violent acting out goes unrestrained. ***The bottom line for us to understand here is the root cause of such behavior is the workings of the spirit of Satan who works in the mind of any person, male or female. Those who allow the evil workings of Satan to be active in them, causes them to be abusive and inflict their rage on others mainly those who are powerless or unable to fight back.***

I can and will give you some physiological understanding of the behaviors of most people who are abusive to their mates in relationships, even to their children. Although throughout this chapter I will attempt to do just that, please keep in mind the statement in the above paragraph. The bottom line for such behavior is the spirit of Satan, whether it is physiological or whatever clinical identities we desire to give these issuers.

When anger escalates out of control, violence and abuse can easily result. The line between what's abusive and what's not is often difficult to determine. Sometimes the line is crossed without either person being totally aware of the transition. It seems clear that Betty was being abused when her husband punched and threw her against the wall. You may ask, what about Joann? Was her husband being abusive when he sat, looked at her and called her the "B-B" word? Or what about Mike's girlfriend who got so angry and threw his plate of food on the floor instead of at him? The truth of the matter is, all these are examples of abuse, one kind or another.

Abuse occurs any time someone is induced to act in a way that they would not otherwise have chosen to act, by violence, threats, or intimidation. Abuse includes not only habitual beatings, but also the occasional slap or shove and even the threat of such behavior.

Sometimes an abusive incident will occur once and never happen again. So it was with Mary Ann, as she described one argument with her husband where she accused him of not caring enough about her as his wife. "You seem to be more concerned about the feelings of these women at church than you are of me." Mary Ann husband was tired from a very hard day at work; at first he tried to involve himself with reading a book in hopes that she would cool off. After a while he became defensive and counter-attacked. As Mary Ann's frustration mounted, she not only lashed out at her husband verbally, but physically as well. Mary Ann's husband caught her hand just as she was about to hit him a second time, and threw her backwards where she fell heavily and hit her head on the coffee table. They both were very horrified and shaken. Now that incident happened more than nine years ago, and Mary Ann reported that the shock of that incident left an indelible mark on their relationship and provided the necessary restraint to ensure that no further violence would occur.

The first time violence occurs, it is usually a shock to the relationship. The victim feels stunned: and asks the question, "How can someone who supposedly love me, treat me this way?" The victim rationalizes that it must have been an exceptional, isolated incident in which he overreacted. The abuser validates this perception, by promising that it will never happen again. Their mate wanting to believe them, searches for what they might have done wrong to cause their abuser to lose control, so that they can avoid triggering them again. In this way they convince themselves that this is not a problem, so they minimize the seriousness of the episode.

In our society, violence is a part of our daily life. Violence includes incidents outside the family as well as within it. As a child we watched cartoons that showed brutal violence between the cartoon characters that seem to do no lasting harm. We could see a cartoon character killed and reborn an average of three to four times in each episode. Our youth, as well as adults, see violence in the media; we have the convenience of playing war games on the Internet that are full of violence that give us great joy.

The three step model that can be described as a pattern that leads to abuse will include (1) the phase of tension building, (2) the explosion or the acute violent episode, and (3) the remorse phase. I have a very good friend who serves as a counselor at Family First Counseling Center. He describes these three steps this way: "During the tension building phase frustration gradually mounts. The spouses often report being aware that things are leading to a blowup. Sometimes the tension becomes so intolerable that the eventual violence is a relief. When the explosion or the acute violent episode occurs, the victim might be pushed, grabbed, held, slapped, shoved, kicked, bitten, choked, punched, hit with an object, threatened or attacked with a knife or a gun. The remorse phase occurs in the period after the violence, when the abuser often feels embarrassed or humiliated about his loss of control. He swears it will never happen again and finds ways to reassure his mate of his devotion."

The family factor can be an important part of this discussion; domestic violence is the abuse that each person may have experienced in his or her own family. As a child, your earliest role models were your parents or grandparents. As a child if you experienced either of them engaged in an abusive relationship, you may have acquired a template for future relationships. You may have learned that anger is most effectively expressed in violence and that violence is useful as a means of influencing or controlling others. Also little girls may have grown up with the learned behavior that your lot in the relationship is to be subjected to such violence.

If you were abused as a child, it is likely that the violence affected how you view yourself. Anytime parents abuse their children, the children can develop a deep belief that they are not very worthwhile as a person. This feeling of unworthiness can contribute to low self-esteem and dependency on others for validation.

Jealousy is another related factor in domestic violence. "I will kill him!" she told me. "I love him too much to let him go, I'd rather see him dead than to see him with another woman!" A dictionary definition cannot begin to describe that desperate cluster of feeling we have characterized as jealousy. This emotion had the power to overwhelm and destroy the most seemingly sound and secure relationship, the most rational person. Just a lost handkerchief was sufficient, and enough cause for a man to murder his faithful and loving wife. What about Jason wife? Medea, She killed their children in a violent revenge, after discovering Jason's love of another woman.

It is usually stated that a man who abused his mate is mentally jealous. If he's dependent on his spouse for all of his emotional needs, then there is that factor of him constantly being terrified that she may be seeing another man or she may leave him for another man. The fear of abandonment underlying jealousy typically provokes irrational suspiciousness and frequent questioning and accusations.

Mental jealousy can also lead to sexual violence. Rape frequently occurs in battering relationships. It is reported that some men force their mate to have sex with them as a way of feeling reassured about their own sexual identity. Some equate physical and psychological abuse with sexual arousal and they desire sex in the aftermath of a beating.

Everyone who cares and loves feels jealousy at one time or another. The essential decision here is whether you will allow your jealousy to become an all-consuming monster, capable of destroying you and those you love, or become a challenge for you to grow in self-respect and personal knowledge. The challenge will rest with you.

ABUSE THAT IS CALLED:

INSTRUMENTAL AGGRESSION

It is reported that one of the most frightening and dangerous types of abuse, which is usually seen in long-term battering relationships, is called "instrumental aggression." In most cases it is noted, that a rush of primitive rage during which the batterer feels out of control accompanies the abuse in each of his violent episodes. Afterwards the batterer may feel embarrassed and remorseful, temporarily upset about his or her behavior and determined to prevent its recurrence. But sometimes the violence is so rewarded that it becomes ingrained as a habitual way of getting what's wanted. The batterer now feels it is no longer simply an out of control rage response, they accept their rage now as a calculated way of gaining a desired reward. The violence becomes "instrumental" in gaining the reward.

The instrumental aggression in a batterer causes him or her to feel that they can beat their mate for no apparent reason and they no longer appear to have any internal feelings of rage. The abuser also appears to show no emotion during their violent episode and show no remorse afterwards. It is also understood that the batterer or abuser is unlikely to give up the habit, even in treatment, since they see it as a justified and useful tactic for getting their needs met.

And so it was in the case of (to protect his identity, let's call him) bro. John. This brother has called or come to my office crying with bruises on this face and parts of his body. It was a shock to see how badly he had been victimized. This violent rage and abuse most of the time was caused by his wife. A few times she has called her two sons to come and beat her husband. He said: "She would do this just to keep me afraid of ever fighting her back." Brother John would tell me: "Many times my wife's anger would get so out of control, I would run out of the house to get away from her hurting me, but she would run down the street after me so I stopped running and let her beat on me." This is a case of Instrumental aggression. In order for brother John's wife to always get her way, she often would proceed with a violent episode of brutal rage upon her husband. He said: "Elder Johnson, I feel so embarrassed to tell you this, but there are times after she had beaten me she would force me to have sex with her. There were times this has happened after she called her two sons to come to our house and beat me. This has been going on for years, and she would not get any help for her aggression." There were a few times I was successful in my many attempts to get brother John's wife to come into my office for counseling. In those few sessions I would meet with brother John and her, and at the end of our session she would express her internal feelings of remorse and embarrassment. During these counseling sessions with them, his wife would also promise to never take out her aggression of anger and rage anymore on her husband, and further promise to seek mental help concerning her anger and aggression. Soon afterward, she discontinued all her sessions of mental counseling and also the medication that was prescribed by her family physician.

After the reoccurrences of this woman's violence and abuse on her husband, she had gotten to the place that she no longer showed any emotion nor felt any remorse for her rage. The batterer now accepts her habitual aggression, as a gaining desired reward. Brother John and his abusive wife had been married for more than forty years. He had always been a gentle, mild and meek mannered person; his behavior has always been the same. He once told me: "I am always afraid of any kind of violence, even violence that is emotional." This past year, brother John died. This brother was well loved and respected my many he was a wonderful man, a man of peace. He will forever be missed.

In our society we think of women as the victims and men as the aggressors in physical or emotional abuse. But that is not true. It is just that most men do not report or even talk about the abuse they endure. Men have been the brunt of jokes forever as being "hen-pecked" those whom are abused by their mates. Some may ask, why would a man who is usually bigger than his spouse let her abuse him?

Such a question as that has many answers. Some men will not try to stop it, because they are afraid of hurting the woman, and there are those who feel if they try to stop their mate's abuse, it will only make them angrier. Then why do they not report it? They are ashamed to report being abused by the woman. In our society, our justice system is more emotionally on the side of the woman than the man. Therefore it takes the word of the women's abuse, than the word of the man's abuse cases. It is just more believable that the aggression was the man. Not the woman.

Men will tolerate more pain and they are more likely to endure the pain rather than cry. And again, many are ashamed to seek medical help for abuse; unless the woman used a weapon (and many do) a woman usually does not have the strength of a man to inflict serious injury like a man can. I know of situations where men have called 911 and when the police arrived they are arrested, instead of the woman because the woman will say the man abused her and the police would not listen when the man tried to tell them that it was the other way around.

There are more and more reported cases of abuse from family members of those who serve in the Military. Those who serve in the military have added factors that contribute to problems with anger and violence. These people are given specific training in the use of violence and combat skills that become part of their day-to-day lives. When the conflict occurs at home, instead of on the battlefield, it's not surprising that violence can result. In addition to the indoctrination process, people in the military and their families also experience a number of other stresses.

Family may be separated for extended periods of time while the man or woman is on tours of duty. The absence of regular contact makes it harder to maintain marital and parental relationships. These factors and so many more can in turn lead to increased isolation, as well as an increased need to feel in control at home. This behavior needs to be in control and it can be one of the most important factors in abusive relationships.

One effect of physical or psychological abuse is the impact it has on the victim's self-esteem. Anytime someone loses the ability to protect him or herself, it can result in constantly feeling afraid and off balance. They become hypervigilent, watching for any sign from their abuser that might lead to anger and beatings. The feeling of being unable to prevent the abuse, the victim often develops a "learned helplessness." After the first violent episode there are many who love their mate and so desperately want the relationship to work out, that they convince themselves that it was a mistake and it won't ever happen again. But it happens again and again. The victim can no longer get away from the fact that their love and trust for their mate has been violated.

If you use alcohol, cocaine or other drugs, it's essential that you understand how these substances contribute to the abusive pattern in which you're involved. And if you are in doubt about the impact that these substances have, then you should go to a treatment center where you can get the assessment and help you need.

Who is responsible for abuse in the relationship? The abuser alone is responsible for the abuse, and unless he or she acknowledges that they have a problem with anger and want to stop their violent behavior, the outlook for them and their relationship is not good. No matter how angry a person gets, there are always alternatives to violence, and their choice of violence is just that: their choice. Even if the abuser feels that they have no other resources in dealing with their anger, they should never use violence to justify their anger.

Can things change in an abusive relationship? There must be a motivation to change. The abuser must acknowledge their problem with the anger and violence. They must show remorse for their abusive episodes and wish to sincerely change enough to work on developing new behaviors. The presence of their remorse is an important indication of motivation, and their willingness to admit their problem and seek professional help to work on it long enough to stop the cycle. Since violence is a behavior that you learned, it follows that you can also learn nonviolent alternatives and problem-solving communication skills as a more positive way of controlling your anger.

FROM THE DESK OF: ELDER G E JOHNSON

How beautiful you are, my darling! Oh, how beautiful! Your eyes behind your veil are doves. Your hair is like a flock of goats descending from mount Gilead. Your teeth are like a fleck of sheep just shorn, coming up from the washing. Each has its twin; not one of them is alone. Your lips are like scarlet ribbon; your mouth is lovely. Your temples behind your veil are like the halves of a pomegranate. Your neck is like the tower of David, built with elegance. On it hangs a thousand shields all of them shields of warriors. Your breasts are, like twin fawns of a gazelle that browse among the lilies.

In today's society we may feel somewhat awkward as we read this intensely private and most intimate praise. These beautiful words are expressed in romantic poetry, which some people actually find difficult to accept as belonging in the Bible. We notice the beautiful imagery as the lovers praise each other. Being from a different culture, the words these lovers are using may seem strange to us. But the intense feeling of their love and admiration for each other is universal. No matter what part of this world we are from, the communicating of love and admiration expressed between lovers can enhance any relationship.

Beautiful words are refreshing. How often do we refresh our mates with words of admiration and love? Do they hear more of complaining, blaming, problems and your unhappiness about one thing or another? We should learn to discuss our complaints at a more agreeable and proper time. Your mate should hear, and would love to hear more words of love. Mates in marriage and relationships should continually work at refreshing each other by acting out and speaking encouraging words. Make a change of pace in the relationship, and surprise your mate with love and gifts.

Lastly, as the word of God would have all to know: God created marriage, God created sex. The reality of sexual intercourse, the physical act of it and the emotional union of male and female, should be a holy means of celebrating their love. Those who are physically able to produce children, and experience the pleasure of love in sexual intercourse, are protected by the commitment of their marriage.

May you be blessed with the richness of God's glory, and may the wonders of His love rest upon you and yours.